Wakefield Press

From Kurmond Kid to Cancer Crusader

Frederick Oscar Stephens AM, MD, MS, FRCS (Ed), FACS, FRACS
Emeritus Professor of Surgery, The University of Sydney
Emeritus Professor of Surgical Oncology, Sydney Hospital and The Royal Prince Alfred Hospital, Sydney.

By the same author

Cancer Explained

All About Prostate Cancer

All About Breast Cancer

The Cancer Prevention Manual

Basics of Oncology

Induction Chemotherapy (in press)

From Kurmond Kid to Cancer Crusader

Fred Stephens

Wakefield Press

Wakefield Press
1 The Parade West
Kent Town
South Australia 5067
www.wakefieldpress.com.au

First published 2011

Cover design by Stacey Zass, page 12
Typeset by Wakefield Press
Printed and bound by Hyde Park Press, Adelaide

National Library of Australia Cataloguing-in-Publication entry

Author:	Stephens, Fred, 1927– .
Title:	From Kurmond kid to cancer crusader / Fred Stephens.
ISBN:	978 1 86254 957 9 (pbk.).
Subjects:	Surgeons – New South Wales – Kurmond – Biography.
	Cancer – Treatment.
Dewey Number:	617.092

Contents

Dedicated
to my parents,
without whose unqualified love and support the work
reported in this book would not have been achieved

Royalties from this book will go towards
the establishment of a
Dorys and Hedley Stephens Chair of Surgical Oncology

Foreword

Karl S. Kruszelnicki

The years 1927 to 2000 were years of great change in Australia. Frederick Stephens grew up in a house without electricity, telephone, running water or sewerage. From this, he grew up to be Professor of Surgery at the University of Sydney – a remarkable achievement.

This book is his story, and provides an insight into his life, and the society in which he lived. It tracks his progress through high school and university, his travels across the globe, his personal life and, yes, his surgical career. Along the way, he helped improve dramatically the treatment of surgical patients with cancer. It is always difficult to bring in change, and Professor Stephens had to work hard to improve his patients' treatments.

Having reached mandatory retirement age, Fred Stephens is now retired. Unfortunately, due to lack of university funding, no successor has been appointed. The university's aiming, and should be in a position, to develop a leading comprehensive cancer centre. Via its teaching hospitals, the University now has excellent medical oncology, radiation oncology, investigation and pathology services headed by eminent Professors. However, without the skills, know-how and knowledge of an experienced and dedicated surgical oncologist, a Cancer Centre would be incomplete and unbalanced.

In writing this book Professor Stephens hopes to draw attention to the need to re-establish an internationally regarded unit in Surgical Oncology headed by a Professor. In the former unit, headed by Fred, Sydney University was a world leader. Re-establishment of such a unit should make it a realistic possibility for Sydney University to establish a universally recognised, truly comprehensive, Cancer Treatment and Research Centre

I first met Professor Stephens when I was a mature-age medical student in one of his classes. I always found him to be most knowledgeable and accessible, even to the most junior students. This is his very personal recount.

Karl S. Kruszelnicki
Julius Sumner Miller Fellow, University of Sydney

Foreword

Professor Earl Owen

Professor Stephens's dedicated career pioneering the scientific, multifaceted treatment of people with locally advanced cancers is now part of medical history. The trials and tribulations that befall pioneers of radical sensible ideas, such as jealousy, pig-headedness and hidden political motives, and how they have been overcome by this courageous and talented surgeon, are now part of this open, very readable story.

In any American or English teaching university surgical department, Professor Stephens's successful clinical advances would have been encouraged and lauded, giving a much earlier improvement for cancer sufferers using his united surgical/medical/scientific and social positive approach.

From tough boyhood years with a struggling big family in a tiny country village, Fred quietly and determinately made it to medical school, and eventually became its talented and beloved cancer treatment pioneering Professor of Surgery. Even then he had to battle on with his desire to help those doomed by their dreaded cancers as his research work and clinically proven results were not accepted, believed or even acknowledged for a long time.

For those willing to look at the illustrations in the 'Clinical Case Supplement', which is appended to the text, the before and after pictures dramatically show how even the most frightening cancer can be tamed and even cured by Fred's logical, multi-skilled approach.

When such a Surgical Oncology Unit is eventually and belatedly formed in Sydney it will owe its existence to a remarkable and humble pioneer, Professor Fred Stephens.

Professor Earl Owen, AO, Leg d'Honneur
Past President, International College of Surgeons

In the beginning God created Kurmond.

Kurmond is a delightful, peaceful village in New South Wales, along the Bell's Line of Road, between Kurrajong and Richmond; it is located northwest of Sydney between the Blue Mountains and the Hawkesbury River.
The name KURMOND was derived from the KUR of Kurrajong and the MOND of Richmond.

Chapter One

From Kurmond Kid to Medical Student

Mum and Dad

My Mum, Dorys Reed, was the daughter of Frederick Reed, an immigrant from Yorkshire, England, who lived in Croydon, New South Wales, with his wife, Sarah Mosman, and their seven surviving children (their first-born had died in infancy). My grandmother, Sarah Mosman, was a member of the Mosman family after which the suburb of Mosman was named. It was in Mosman that I came to live and raise my family in my later life. Frederick Reed was originally a shopkeeper who bought a small bakery, which he developed and later became a highly regarded Master Baker. He was a devout Christian and a Methodist lay preacher. Mum was their third of eight children. She had a wonderful sense of humour. She frowned on vulgarity or hurtful humour but otherwise she could see a funny side to almost anything. I feel sure that this is what kept her well-balanced and able to continue in good spirits in spite of what might have been an impossibly burdensome life. Her motto was 'If you can't say anything good about someone then better not to say anything at all'. She often quoted the Christian ethic: 'Do unto others as you would have them do unto you.'

She trained as a secretary and was working with her own father in the bakery business when she became engaged to my father. Their two families had been friends for years and both families attended the same Sunday school and church in the western Sydney suburb, Croydon. They were also in the same tennis club.

Mum always had a medicine chest at the ready, full of bandages, a sling, ointments, 'tonics', and mixtures of various kinds for health problems. She always had something to give us if we had a cough, cold, tummy-ache, an injury or any other health problem. Particular remedies since passed into history were 'Bate's salve' a dirty brown ointment that was heated and dropped hot onto an infected wound; 'Bidomack' a tonic for anyone who was off his or her food or otherwise not looking well; castor oil for anyone constipated or with a tummy-ache; and 'Ung-Vita' ointment, which came in a round tin that would heal any wound or sore. I never understood how it worked but when Mum rubbed butter onto a head that had been hurt in a fall, it would soon feel better. Of course there was also 'Bonnington's Irish Moss' containing 'petrol-oxymal of carogene from a seaweed found on the coast of Ireland', which was given as a cure for any cough, cold or sore throat. She would also make the inevitable 'bread-poultice' which, if applied hot, would draw pus from and cure a boil or any other infected wound. It all seemed very effective at the time, but I now believe the cures lay in her love and attention as well as the realisation that a second dose of treatment would be inevitable if we did not feel better.

My parents had been sweethearts for years when Dad, aged twenty-one, formally asked my mother's father for her hand in marriage. He was the son of William Stephens, government printer, who lived in Burwood, New South Wales, with his wife, Matilda Stark. He was the sixth and youngest son of a family of eight (six boys and two girls). Shortly after his engagement to my mother, war broke out and he enlisted in the army and in December, 1915, was sent overseas with the Australian Infantry Forces (AIF).

After leaving Australia Dad had further training in Egypt where he met up with his cousin and best friend, Stanley Stark, who was to be best man at his wedding. Although they were in different battalions they both held the rank of corporal. Sadly that was the last time they were to see each other. In 1916 both battalions were transferred to Northern France where they served on the battlefields of Flanders and the Somme.

In a battle at Fleurbaix, near Armentières, Dad was severely injured trying to save his superior officer who was lying dying in no-man's-land between the two battlefields. His superior officer had been drinking heavily and had gone out into no-man's-land 'to inspect the trenches'. He was lying unconscious and badly injured by shellfire when Dad went out to try to bring him back. The officer died on the battlefield and Dad, severely injured and lying unconscious, was taken prisoner.

This episode was recorded in Charles Bean's official history of the war series. Incidentally, horrible as it was to be a prisoner of war, Dad always gave credit to the German doctors who saved his life. He said that he was treated in a hospital ward with injured German soldiers and was given equally good treatment. In fact an injured German officer was in the next bed and a German corporal, who could write English, wrote a letter on Dad's behalf home to his fiancée and family. He was held prisoner of war in Gefangenenlager, Dulmen 1, Westfalen, Germany for two years.

Medical records indicated that Dad had multiple shrapnel injuries to his head, one eye, jaw, chest, a shoulder, hand, hip, leg and one foot – a total of 16 shrapnel wounds – the most severe being to his head with shrapnel embedded in his brain.

His two best mates, his cousin Stanley Stark, and my mother's cousin, Oscar Clark were both killed in one battle. Thereafter Dad had hatred not for the Germans but for alcohol (he would not allow any alcohol into our house). He always expressed gratitude and admiration for the German medical team that brought him in and cared for him as well as they could under the circumstances after he had been given up for dead. It was through similar such experiences of other soldiers that the propaganda stories of the 'savagery and cruelty of those inhuman German Huns' were seen to be just that: propaganda. The Germans, like the allied soldiers, were just young men under orders who were fighting for a cause.

Dad rarely spoke of his years in a prisoner of war camp but we did discover something of his rehabilitation and hobby activities when we found a scarf and some socks that he had knitted from threads of worn-out clothing using sticks as knitting needles.

He always set a wonderful example in good manners. He would never allow us to start eating a meal before Mum was ready to start and he always held out a chair for her, or any other woman, before being seated himself. Grace was always said either by Dad or Mum before meals. Dad always raised his hat to a lady and would always walk on the outside (the roadside) of the footpath when walking with Mum. Such manners were originally developed to protect women and their clothing from mud or dust being splashed on them from passing horse-drawn carts or motorcars on the roads. He would also always offer his seat to a lady or an elderly man standing in a crowded bus or train. He would never go through a door before a woman; he would hold the door open for her and I never heard a swearword in our home.

To say that Dad liked a 'cuppa tea' would be a masterly understatement. He liked a cup as soon as he got up in the morning, at breakfast time, at morning and afternoon tea time, with lunch and with dinner, before going anywhere, as soon as he got back from anywhere, whenever friends arrived, whenever friends stayed for more than an hour, whenever friends left, and whenever he had nothing else to do. Other than those times he never had one unless he was thirsty!

When he returned from the war he and Mum were married in the Malvern Hill Methodist church, Croydon, in October 1919. Although he had been trained as an electrician pre-war, he joined his father-in-law in a new bakery business, 'Reed and Stephens'. However, his war injuries – especially the head injuries that caused him to have epileptic fits (starting two or three years later) – made it unsafe for him to work as a baker or to drive the new car he bought with his service discharge money. He was retired to a small soldier settlement farm in Kurmond. The car was also retired to rest and rust in the backyard of a garage workshop in North Richmond. Years later when we passed that garage on the old Kurrajong to Richmond train, 'Pansy', Dad would point out the remains of his old 'Talbot' motorcar amongst the junk in the garage. Until recently I had always believed the car was a 'Talbot', which was a prestigious English car, but photographs of the car clearly show that it was a 'T' model Ford.

Both Mum and Dad lived for their children. They were so very proud of everything we did, sometimes, especially in Dad's case, it was almost embarrassing.

After World War I

When we first lived in Kurmond, Dad had an orange orchard (most of the district was orange orchards), but soon the Great Depression was upon us. I have memories of the farmers trying to sell boxes of oranges along the Bell's Line of Road, and others earning their subsistence money by building roads and dams using horse-drawn scoops and drays. This subsistence payment was equivalent to present-day 'work for the dole' and it did result in good roads, railways and other public utilities being established.

It soon became obvious, though, that Dad was not well enough to farm so the orange trees were removed and Dad was fully retired as a 'totally and permanently incapacitated soldier' living solely on a war-service TPI pension. We kept a couple of cows in the paddock for milk, and some chooks in the chook-yard but that was all. Dad's health was always a worry; he often fell into a fit (about once a week) and suffered injuries, and we all learned what to do when he was having one. I once had to help pull him off a railway line. Dad was a kind man but the day after he had had a fit he was like a bear with a sore head for about 24 hours – we knew to keep away from him. In a way, I benefited from this experience: I was so impressed by the attention that Dr Steel of Richmond always gave to Dad. Dr Steel would always come so readily from Richmond if he was needed, and Mum knew that if ever he was not available (which I don't think was ever the case) Dr Arnold of Windsor would come to help.

Looking back now from the vantage of my own old age I realise with sadness and regret how little I knew about my father's World War I experiences – experiences that so profoundly shaped the story of his adult life and in turn shaped mine. He accepted his disabilities without bitterness or complaint and spoke very little about his wartime and POW experiences.

It was not until later in life that I began to understand his bravery in the battlefields and his uncomplaining acceptance of his severe injuries, especially the head injuries that resulted in life-long epilepsy that he also accepted as limiting his way of life thereafter.

I remember visiting him in hospital on about three occasions. One particular occasion when I must have been about 3 or 4 years old was after he had fallen in a fit and suffered several injuries including a broken jaw. His face was swollen and heavily bandaged. On another occasion when I was 6 or 7 years old I remember helping my Mum pull him off a railway line after he had fallen in a fit onto a railway track. Luckily there was no train coming at the time. He accepted all these consequences of battle without complaint.

These experiences made me more and more certain that I wanted to be a doctor one day. To be able to make sick people better and to help comfort their families would be the best job in the world. This belief became even stronger when my little sister Dolly became ill with scarlet fever. She was hospitalised in isolation and not allowed to touch or be touched by any of her family or friends. A few months later, at only four years of age, she died leaving my Mum and Dad terribly broken-hearted. Many years later I met Sir Howard, later Lord Florey, the great Australian doctor/scientist responsible for preventing scarlet fever ever causing such tragedies again by his discovery of the clinical use of penicillin. I felt very honoured but at the same time it was sad to realise that if only this had been discovered about thirty-five years earlier Dolly could have been saved.

When I was about five years old my parents bought me a little 'doctor's bag' with a little red cross on it in which I kept bandages, dressings and various lotions and ointments. The bag and contents were inevitably used when any one of my brothers or sisters, but especially one of our pet animals, had a cut or other injury. From that time on the thought of being anything else but a doctor never occurred to me.

Our home, in Longleat Lane, Kurmond, had three small bedrooms, a kitchen with fuel stove and oven, a dining/lounge/music room, a bathroom, and verandas; across the yard there was a shed which housed a toolshed, woodheap, laundry, stables and 'dunny'. The shed was made of vertically erected split ironbark logs. Longleat Lane has since been upgraded from dirt to a bitumen surface road with many more houses, so its name has been upgraded to the more sophisticated Longleat Road.

In 1927 when our family moved to Kurmond I was three weeks old. Joyce was six, Heather five, Stan three and Evelyn one. Dolly, Bruce and Elaine were still to come; but when they arrived they were the only real 'Kurmonders'.

We loved our home and our devoted parents. How Mum and Dad managed with all the children, Dad's war injuries, and the Great Depression, we will never know. I am sure their deep religious faith and deep love for each other had a lot to do with it.

When first we lived in Kurmond there was no electricity, no

telephone and no laid-on water or sewerage. We lived and studied by candlelight and kerosene lamps, and communicated by seeing and talking to people in person or writing letters and putting them in the post. Letters took several days to or from Sydney; we collected them from the little post office up the hill. Dad would walk up the hill every day (except Sunday) to collect any letters, and buy the *Sydney Morning Herald* and groceries from Mr Merriman's shop (the village's only shop). Mum cooked on our wood-fuelled stove or in the oven. If we just wanted to boil water for the regular cups of tea or boil eggs, we did it on a kerosene primus stove. We made toast on a toasting fork in front of the wood fire. The toast made this way really tasted like toast should taste, thick with butter or dripping if we hadn't any butter or jam, and real cream.

We loved the rain: hearing it on the tin roof was great and a few days later we would always find and pick the inevitable mushrooms that followed the rain. The memory of eating those wild field mushrooms on toast still makes my mouth water.

In our little old home some things were immutable. Mum did the washing on Mondays after scrubbing the most soiled clothes on a wooden washing-board, then boiling the washing in water with Siren or Sunlight soap in the copper set over a wood fire, and stirring the clothes in the boiling water with a wooden clothes-stick before hanging it out on wire clothes lines supported by clothes-forks. She rinsed the whites in water with a 'blue bag', apparently to make them more sparkling white! She did the ironing on Tuesdays, using a flat iron heated on the stove. Wednesdays were Mum's 'mending and sewing days' when she replaced any missing buttons, patched or mended any worn or damaged clothes, and darned socks using a mushroom-shaped sock holder that kept the sock in place with its hole exposed. She thoroughly cleaned the house on Thursdays (using a broom, a mop, a carpet sweeper and, when necessary, a can of floor stain with a brush). Fridays were kept for writing up the minutes of the church Sunday school and Kurmond School parents and citizens meetings of which she always seemed to be the secretary. Saturdays she spent with us kids, and Dad, sometimes playing tennis, having a picnic or going for bush walks. She spent Sundays teaching and playing the piano at Sunday school, going to church, where she played the organ, and preparing our big Sunday roast dinner that was usually shared with the church minister. All this with our disabled father and seven children to care for! She and Dad were never interested in accumulating wealth, fame or power, only in doing the best they could for their family, their community and their country.

Our home was heated by an open wood-fire in the dining/lounge/music room and we opened the windows if we wanted 'air-conditioning'. In summer this always let blowflies into the house and these were partly controlled by liberal use of a fly swatter. Dad was the expert in this. Flies were also caught on 'sticky tapes' hung from a kerosene lamp attached to the ceiling (in the kitchen), or directly from the ceiling in other rooms. There was a saying in Kurmond that the best time to go to 'the dunny' was when cabbage was being cooked in the kitchen; all the blowflies would be in the kitchen.

Radio was in its infancy and I remember my big brother, Stan, making a crystal-set radio. He and I would sit by the fire under the copper in the laundry on cold winters' nights trying to listen to the test cricket 'being broadcast from England'. Like everyone else we later learned that it was regularly faked by broadcasters in a Sydney studio. As it was played in England cricket information was constantly cabled to Sydney where the commentators pretended it was actually happening in front of them. The sound of a bat hitting a ball was made by the broadcaster's pencil being jabbed on a paper pad.

Some years later a new era of entertainment was introduced into our world when Dad bought a real radio. What fun it was in those early days, not only did we listen to sport (I can remember hearing Don Bradman make his world-record-breaking triple century) we were also introduced to a wonderful era of fun radio serials including 'Dad and Dave', 'Ada and Elsie', 'Mrs 'Arris and Mrs Iggs' and later 'Mrs 'Obbs' and 'Yes Wot' with Greenbottle. Our other family favourites on Sunday nights were the radio serial 'Doctor Mac' and 'World Famous Tenors'.

In those days it seemed that everybody sang; it wasn't restricted to the professional few. Singing was a means of family entertainment. It was cost-free, unwired, unplugged and completely joyous. We always had a piano that we would sing around while Mum, or later my sister Evelyn, played. One day Dad bought a wind-up gramophone that played '78' records. My favourite records were 'The Teddy Bears' Picnic', which I was given as a special birthday present, 'Laughing Ginger Brown' and 'I was a gay Caballero, returning from Rio de Janeiro'. I confess that I do find it hard to adjust to the amplified soundtracks of today, especially when the sound of instruments drowns the lyrics of the vocalist.

For other family entertainment we played cards, especially in front of the kitchen or dining-room fire on cold winter's nights – and winters were cold in Kurmond. On Saturdays and on school holidays, but never on the Sabbath Day, Dad and whoever was around often played cricket on the dirt road. Our wicket was a fruit box or a kerosene tin, and our ball was made of stone-hard composite material (seemingly like iron coated concrete), not the more expensive and relatively softer 'six stitcher' leather balls used today. Every time one of the locals, Mr Cook, came speeding past we had to stop play and take our wicket off the road in a hurry. Mr Cook, who was clearly wealthy, owned the only car in Kurmond, although our neighbour, Mr Downs, eventually bought a utility truck for his farm.

When we were a little older and had saved enough Saturday pennies (we were given a penny pocket money every Saturday), we sometimes caught Mr Franks's lorry (a covered truck) to the Saturday 'flicks' in Richmond. We especially loved films starring Buck Rogers, Hopalong Cassidy, Tom Mix or Abbott and Costello, and of course the next episode of the Saturday night serial that had finished the previous week at an exciting, critical or threatening juncture.

As would be expected from their family backgrounds, Mum and Dad were both devout Christians. They believed there was something seriously missing from their lives and our lives without a church or Sunday school in the village, so they started church services and a Sunday school in our home and made plans to have a church built on their property.

Our first Sunday school superintendent was a Seventh Day Adventist pastor, Reverend Maunder. It was a true ecumenical act to have a Seventh Day Adventist pastor as superintendent of a Methodist Sunday School. I remember Mr Maunder giving me a special prize for reciting the 23rd Psalm when I was five years old.

Up until a little wooden church was built on a corner of our land, Sunday school classes were held on our verandah, and church services held in our dining-room. The church minister from Windsor, or a student minister or a lay preacher from the Hawkesbury Agricultural College, Dr Harrison, usually stayed for dinner.

In those days, the term 'sex discrimination' had not been invented. The boys had most of the outdoor jobs and the girls were mostly indoors helping Mum with the housework. Dad, Stan, Bruce (once he was big enough) and I pumped the water from the well. The water was rainwater collected from the house roof and the shed roof. The well water had to be hand-pumped to the elevated tank on four thick, tree-trunk stilts. Mum became the luckiest mum in Kurmond because she had the luxury of having water piped from the tank above sink-level into the kitchen, laundry and bathroom. To pump the water from the well up to the elevated tank was a regular job. Our 1000-gallon water tank became a distinctive landmark that could be seen for miles around and it gave us a warm glow of pride when it first came into sight after we had been away for any length of time. Sadly, after standing for more than 70 years, the tank and the well have been removed. Our large round concrete well with its concrete top approximately a metre above ground level was also a distinctive feature. On very hot days we would drop a kerosene tin bucket attached to a rope down the well, and draw up water that was always refreshingly cool; but we inevitably shared our bathwater and often our drinking water with mosquito wrigglers. 'Never mind the wrigglers in the drinking water,' Dad would say. 'They are only a bit of extra meat.'

We also had to feed the chooks. The female chickens were kept for laying eggs and, in a clear case of sex discrimination, only one lucky male rooster was kept to help the hens make more chickens. The other roosters were dispassionately fattened up for Christmas or a special Sunday meal.

One boy's job, for which I don't think the girls ever demanded equal opportunity, was 'burying the dunny cans'. Our dunny (toilet) furniture consisted of a kerosene tin under a wooden-plank bench with a bottom-sized hole in it. Whenever the can was full, one of the male members of the family had to dig a hole somewhere in the garden or in the paddock, tip the contents in it and cover the hole with dirt. Strangely enough we didn't seem to mind doing it. I liked it because one of my favourite hobbies was my garden and my vegetables; my favourite blue gladioli flowers always grew well wherever a dunny can had been buried. It was a case of the original organically grown food and flowers. After World War II Kurmond went upmarket: our kerosene tins were replaced by specifically designed round 'dunny cans' that were collected on a weekly basis by a council 'night-cart man'.

We all loved our home and liked keeping it looking good. I adopted 'home maintenance' as a bit of a hobby. I played all games but was not interested in competitive sport, politics or reading novels. I was always interested in making things, especially finding out how things worked, including how medical things worked. I remember persuading my parents to buy some paint when the house started to look shabby. They did, and I painted the whole of the exterior of the house including the roof, which I painted blue, my favourite colour, to make it different to the unpainted iron roofs or the painted red tin roofs in the village. I also remember persuading my parents to buy some bags of cement so that I could concrete the dirt floor of the laundry. This made the laundry more comfortable for Mum. As well as handyman tasks I also enjoyed singing, especially in church or when milking the cows, distressing though it might have been to neighbours, the cows or anyone within hearing range.

There was no such thing as sex education in those days either. I don't know how my brothers or sisters got their sex education but it certainly was not from Mum or Dad. Anything they may have told me about the birds and the bees I must have misunderstood. Lots of flowers and some vegetables grew wild around our house, especially cosmos, nasturtiums and pumpkin vines, and I remember as a four-year-old catching bees in pumpkin flowers, holding them there and waiting for them to make honey. It was disappointing. There was never any honey. However, hiding in the cosmos bushes was where the girls across the road taught me something more relevant about the birds and the bees. We knew what we were doing was 'naughty' but we didn't know why and certainly found it interesting. Despite learning of the anatomical difference between boys and girls, I remained unenlightened as to the implications until the chooks and cows put on their demonstrations.

Whether we needed it or not, as we often thought we didn't, we all had a bath once a week, on Saturdays. The girls' bath time was first, followed by the boys, using the same tub of water, since it was predictable that the boys would be dirtier than the girls. Rainwater was scarce and precious. The bathwater was heated in the laundry copper and carried in kerosene tins into the bathroom. After our baths, the bathwater was always put on the garden, yet somehow the garden survived. One day Dad bought a bathroom chip-heater in which water was heated in a double-walled tank with a wood fire in the middle. It sputtered and steamed impatiently when the bathwater had boiled and was ready.

It was about that time that Mum became especially blessed by having her old wooden laundry washtubs replaced by two beautiful new modern concrete washtubs with a new 'wringer' on the bridge between them. The wringer consisted of a pair of wooden rollers turned by a handle so that wet washing from one tub passed between the rollers to the other tub by turning the handle. Thus the soaking-wet washing became squeeze-semi-dried. This saved Mum from hand-wringing all the washing before hanging it out on the washing-line.

Another item of 'luxury' laundry equipment was the 'mangle'. The mangle also consisted of two heavy wooden rollers turned by a handle, but the rollers were much bigger and heavier than the wringer rollers. The 'mangle' was used to semi-flatten out the bed sheets or tablecloths after they had been dried on the washing-line. This saved having to iron the bed sheets but Mum still ironed the tablecloths. There were no drip-dry sheets or drip-dry anything else in those days. All cotton materials looked very rough and crinkled after they had dried on the washing line. The mangle was heavy and difficult to turn, so one of us would help Mum or Dad do this job. It also needed to be used carefully. My brother Bruce once held a sheet for too long and one of his fingers was caught in the mangle. He had one slightly deformed finger for the rest of his life.

The greatest sadness in our lives in the early days was the death of our then youngest sister Dolly, 'little Dolly Dimples', when she was only four years old. Dolly died from after-effects of scarlet fever. Scarlet fever is an infectious disease which in those days was treated in the isolation hospital then known as 'The Coast Hospital', later converted to a general hospital and called the Prince Henry Hospital. For reasons I did not understand, the children in that hospital had to have their heads shaved and were kept in isolation. (I have recently been advised by a senior physician that all children in an infectious ward had their hair shaved off because of a belief that infections, including scarlet fever, may have been transmitted by head lice. We now know this is not the case.) I remember visiting Dolly with Mum and Dad and the rest of my brothers and sisters, but we were kept some distance away from her and could only wave to her. Poor little kiddie, just four years old in bed with her head shaved and not allowed to have her mum or dad or anyone else give her a cuddle. It was heartbreaking. When she was eventually discharged from hospital she had a condition then known as 'dropsy' which is now recognised as heart failure. Dolly was bed-ridden for some weeks, all the time becoming weaker and weaker. One day she said to Mum, 'Mummy I'm tired'. In her mother's arms she closed her eyes and fell asleep – forever.

I don't think Mum or Dad ever recovered from the death of Dolly. I took Dolly's loss very hard too because being close in age, just one year apart, Dolly had been my special sibling playmate.

Early school years

We all had our primary school education in the two-roomed, two-teacher Kurmond School. In those days most classes had a Stephens in them. Every Christmas the school had a Christmas party and dance with the 'real' Santa Claus in attendance. Everyone walked to school no matter what the weather but we in the Stephens family were lucky, school was less than a mile from home. Other kids had to walk two miles or more. Our primary school was a two-roomed weatherboard building with a shed and two dunnies, one for the girls and one for the boys. The dunnies were of the most basic type with a big deep pit under a wooden plank with a round hole in it.

One of the classrooms was for 1st, 2nd and 3rd classes together, with one young lady teacher (Miss Stark followed later by Miss Johnstone) and the other was for 4th, 5th and 6th classes where the teacher was Mr Armstrong, the headmaster. On reflection they were very good teachers but how they managed three classes at a time is still a mystery to me. I still remember Miss Stark teaching us the letters of the alphabet and putting them together to make the words 'fat', 'cat' 'mat' and 'sat' then putting them together in sentences like 'the fat cat sat on a rag mat'. We did not have pencils and paper; we drew on slates with slate pencils. The only teaching props the teachers had were chalk and a blackboard.

I remember learning the arithmetic tables by repetition and rote learning and English by the use of strict grammar with nouns, verbs, adjectives, conjunctions, prepositions, present and past participles, subjunctive moods etc. Mr Armstrong was strict on grammatical construction, and required correct use of subjective or objective pronouns, correct use of present and past participles, correct use of collective nouns as singular, correct pronunciation, the difference between the use of 'most' or 'the majority' and the difference between proper nouns and common nouns. Unfortunately, try as he did, Mr Armstrong failed to make me a good 'speler'.

We only wore shoes to school on special occasions, but clean hands and fingernails and a certain discipline were essential. After the school bell rang, we had to 'line up' in two rows. Then we responded to the headmaster's demand to 'show hands', then 'show backs of hands'. Hands and nails were inspected. Anyone with dirty hands or fingernails was sent to make this good before beginning classes. Every Monday morning the Australian flag was raised and we all saluted and repeated the words: 'I honour my God, I serve my king, I salute my flag'.

It was during primary school that I first thought I had fallen in love. The object of my affections was Ruth Higgins, a classmate, who to me was beautiful. However, I was sure she would not be interested in someone a little younger than her, so my puppy love was never revealed to anyone, especially not to Ruth. I would just look at her and wish I had the courage to say more than 'hello Ruth'.

In 2005 Kurmond School celebrated its 85th anniversary. The first person to greet me there was the same Ruth Higgins, now a mature-aged woman with her husband and son. I confessed to her that I had been in love with her all through primary school but it had taken all these years for me to pluck up the courage to tell her. An old schoolmate, Cliff Simmons, standing next to me confessed 'I was too, and I wasn't game to tell her either'.

High school

To get to high school we walked a couple of miles through the bush to catch the train, 'Pansy', to Richmond where there was a three-year intermediate Rural High School. Rural schools taught agriculture, technical drawing, woodwork and metalwork (wonderful education for a country kid); but no foreign languages, which, at that time, were necessary for full high school and university education. To catch the train to Richmond after our two mile (3.2 kilometre) walk through the bush, we climbed up a ladder onto the train at a stop in the bush until one day the local community decided to build a real railway platform for Pansy at Thompson's Ridge. Pansy mostly travelled through bushland but in Richmond the train line was along the side of a street between the footpath and the road. She was withdrawn from service in the 1950s and much of the railway track was sold to developers.

I began high school at Richmond Rural School in 1939. The war and my high school years covered the same period so many of our high school activities were limited or modified by many aspects of the war effort.

At high school I liked woodwork, metalwork, technical drawing, botany and agriculture, and still appreciate having studied them, but by then I was sure I wanted to be a doctor and I discovered that Latin was a compulsory subject for entry to medical school. Therefore, when I was thirteen years old, towards the end of my second high school year, my parents arranged for me to leave Richmond Rural School and enrol in an intermediate high school in Homebush where I could study Latin. How they managed financially I will never know, but they found an old family friend, an elderly widow, who agreed to have me as a boarder in her Croydon home. From Croydon I caught a train to school in Homebush.

I was very homesick and always counted the days until the weekend when I would go home to Kurmond to be with my parents and family. My poor mum was landed with my week's washing to do on the weekend but at least I had learned one useful thing: to keep my trousers pressed I put them under my mattress each night and slept on them. They were the days when trousers were made of wool and needed regular pressing to look tidy; there were no synthetics or drip-drys. I got into the habit of pressing my trousers by sleeping with them under the mattress for years after.

Homebush was then only an intermediate high school (it had classes up to third year only, equivalent to today's Year 10). As it was necessary to have a full five years of high school education to matriculate to university, I needed to find a full high school prepared to take a country boy who had learned Latin but not French (French was the standard language at full high schools). Fortunately, because my grades in all subjects were high, the headmaster at Sydney Boys High School (a highly selective school) agreed to enrol me. My parents found me inexpensive boarding digs with another elderly widowed lady who had three or four country boys boarding with her in Kingsford, a few miles by tram from Sydney Boys High School.

Boarding at Kingsford

In our Kingsford boarding house all of the boys became good friends. We were all in more or less in the same boat; our parents could not afford fees for a boarding school, so it was a cheap boarding house or nothing. Our landlady ran her boarding house as cheaply as possible, which meant food for growing young men was always in very limited supply. When we had saved enough pennies, we would buy and eat a loaf of bread, without butter or jam, to keep our hunger at bay. Our landlady was a very thin woman but she had a well-nourished dog that was fed well on meaty bones. We would take it in turns to feed the dog, fighting the dog for the most-meaty scraps.

We all lost weight while living in that boarding house, but I was the luckiest one. The homes of the other boys were hundreds of miles from Sydney so they could only go home in school holidays. My home in Kurmond was little more than a two-hour train ride from Sydney so I was able to go home every weekend. On weekends my brother Bruce and I loved to show off and demonstrate our horse-riding skills to the city folk who came to Mrs Carter's riding school, which was near our home. We loved horse-riding and shared that passion with two of my Sydney High classmates, Victor and Bob Humphries, who also lived on a farm in Lower Portland, a village on the Hawkesbury River not far from Kurmond. Vic and Bob studied dentistry at the same time as I studied medicine. We have retained lifelong friendships.

Discovering girls

A new picture theatre had been built at Kurrajong, and Dierdre, a thirteen-year-old visitor, invited me to go to 'the pictures' with her. We were sitting holding hands in the back row of the cinema when quite suddenly, out of the blue, Dierdre slapped the most passionate open-mouthed kiss on my lips. I really didn't know what was happening except that I liked it. It was a kiss to remember but it was disappointing to learn the next day that Dierdre had returned to Sydney with her parents. Unhappily, that was the last I ever saw or heard of her. Perhaps it was just as well.

At the age of eleven or twelve, I remember being invited to have sex in the bush with a girl in my class; but the teaching of my home, Sunday school and church told me it was wrong, so I declined. I had a similar invitation when I was a twelve or thirteen year old by a girl classmate at Richmond school. Again I resisted the temptation.

At Sydney Boys High School and boarding in Kingsford with a bunch of country boys, there was a lot of talk about sex. I decided that I should have a condom just in case I might 'get lucky' one day. Nervous as a kitten, I went into the local pharmacy determined to buy a condom but expecting to be served by the male chemist. Unfortunately a girl behind the counter served me so, quite embarrassed, my courage left me and I bought some toothpaste instead. So I waited for a day when only the chemist was behind the counter. When I could see that only he was in the shop, I bravely went to the counter, but he asked his young female assistant to come to the counter to serve me. My bravado instantly vanished and again I asked for toothpaste. Eventually I found another chemist shop with only a male chemist serving: 'It's for my big brother who is married,' I explained.

The first time I lost some control over my sexual impulses was during my first year of medical school when an old country schoolmate and I were boarding with a widowed lady in Bondi. We discovered that the sixteen-year-old girl next-door took a bath every night at 7 pm. Her bathroom was opposite ours and she always left her window open, so my friend, Alan, and I regularly took up our positions at our bathroom window at 7 pm. Our dinner was always ready at 7.30 pm but if it so happened that the object of our interest was a few minutes late for her bath Alan and I were always a little late for dinner. I used to say to Alan that as a medical student I was justified in taking an interest in the study of anatomy of a young woman but as he was studying for an arts degree there was no such justification for him other than that he must have been a sexual pervert.

University studies

The very year that I enrolled in the University of Sydney Faculty of Medicine it was announced that Latin was no longer a prerequisite so my years of Latin study were suddenly irrelevant. Still my ambition to be a doctor was to be fulfilled and I have found my knowledge of Latin to be very useful in understanding medical and anatomical terminology.

I know that somehow my parents would have supported me in attending university but it was a considerable help when I was awarded one of the state's 200 exhibitions or bursaries which paid my university fees. With this and by taking weekend and holiday jobs, the costs of boarding away from home during my university days became acceptable. In addition, working different holiday jobs was a great experience in itself.

If I was in Kurmond for weekends and short vacations I mostly did farm jobs but if I was in Sydney I worked in my uncles' (Reed and Sons) bakery. In the summer long vacation I took a different holiday job each time. As a seventeen-year-old, in between finishing school and commencing at medical school, I got a job as a storeman and packer in a Sydney Woolworths shop. I still have a reference from my boss that states that I was a very good storeman and packer. It was here where I met my first serious girlfriend, Pat, a pretty sixteen-year-old blonde who was working in Woolworths as a shop assistant during her high school long vacation. Pat took me home to meet her parents and when she took me for a walk to show me her father's garden and garden shed she also showed me what stimulating and cuddlesome anatomical flesh could be found on the upper part of a young woman's chest. At least until her father demanded that we come out of his shed and advised me in no uncertain terms that I would remain healthier and less mutilated if I discontinued my association with his daughter.

It was in my fifth year of medicine that I met my first long-term love, Peggy. Peggy was eighteen and I was three years older. I took her home to meet my family in Kurmond and everyone loved her. However, her deeply religious family did not think that I should go on dating their daughter unless we married. Having had a number of different girlfriends I had apparently in their eyes developed something of a reputation as a womaniser. As I was a poor medical student so much wanting to be a doctor and in no position to get married the romance came to a sad end. I don't think that I ever stopped loving Peggy.

My six years of medical school education were not brilliant but very satisfactory. I adopted a policy of doing sufficient study to pass examinations comfortably but not to overdo it to a degree that might deplete my social life. My enjoyment of friends, male as well as female, remained uncompromised. Also, I did not allow my studies to interfere with my love of returning to family, friends and hobbies, especially horses, in Kurmond.

Sydney Hospital

My student clinical years were spent with a number of friends, especially my two old Sydney High School classmates, and subsequently lifelong friends, Len Fienberg and Colin Jennings, in Australia's oldest and greatest hospital at the time, Sydney Hospital. Sydney Hospital is in Macquarie Street, the equivalent of Harley Street in London, and enjoyed a highly prized reputation as the address of the state's best medical specialists. It was highly selective in appointing the best specialists to its staff but it was older and smaller than most teaching hospitals and had a reputation for friendliness and happiness between students, patients and staff.

I enjoyed my student days there and my greatest ambition was to become a member of the hospital's staff one day. I was especially interested in surgery because of my love of doing things with my hands and seeing a good result more or less immediately. Still, trying to be realistic, I believed that I would probably have to settle for my next ambition, which was to be a surgeon in a country town and retain some affiliation with specialist colleagues at Sydney Hospital.

In my final year of medical school my grandmother became very ill, so my parents came to live full-time with her to help care for her. I thought they had left Kurmond temporarily but, unknown to me as they had not wanted to worry me in my final year studies, they had decided to sell our Kurmond home and arranged to buy a new home in Sydney. They wanted to be closer to Grandma and their children, all of whom were now living in Sydney. I was very sad when I learned that we no longer had our home in Kurmond. In fact, for years afterwards I had a recurring dream that I had arrived 'home' in Kurmond only to find it was no longer our home. To this day I still sometimes have that dream.

Final year medical exams were in October and November 1950. In January 1951, I began as a junior doctor, known officially as an intern or resident medical officer (RMO), at the Royal South Sydney Hospital, a hospital then associated with Sydney Hospital. My parents were so proud. It was wonderful to see their happiness after all they had done to help me fulfil my ambition to become a doctor.

Life as a resident medical officer (RMO)

I had not realised how busy life would be working as an RMO, nor did I realise how much I would learn through taking on responsibility for the care of patients day and night. The working days were long – 24 hours on duty, day and night, catching a few hours sleep when possible, with every second weekend off. We were available for our in-patients day and night for twelve consecutive days including duty in the casualty/emergency department one night every week. With such practical commitment to our work we learnt very quickly the application of our six years of medical studies. With three RMO friends who had been in my Sydney Hospital student group, Ken Cooke, Tony Jones and George James, and a very respected senior RMO named Toby Bowering, I lived happily in the resident doctors' quarters of the hospital with free board and lodging (every morning it was cold fried eggs and cold toast for breakfast). Tony, George and I were intrigued by Ken's habit of putting tomato sauce over everything he ate. His eggs for breakfast were always smothered with the red sauce, as was whatever we were served for lunch or dinner. I am sure Ken just liked the taste, but fifty years later medical research has shown that the red colouring matter of tomatoes contains an ingredient called 'lycopene' which has some anti-cancer properties. I last saw Ken at our fifty-five years since graduation celebration, and am pleased to report that he had never had a cancer.

The long hours were repaid by the satisfaction and interest that came from such an incomparably interesting learning experience. I think I learnt more in that year than in all six years of medical school, at least in regards to the more practical aspects of patient care. Our jobs required us to make decisions about diagnosis and care of our patients and justify our decisions to our seniors. There was no excuse for not knowing something; what we did not know we had to look up and learn. Overall we had primary responsibility for our patients, but someone was always around to help if needed and we were well supervised by highly qualified honorary medical staff.

It was in this hospital that I performed my first surgical operations, assisted by one of the senior surgeons. These included my first tonsillectomy, first appendicectomy, and some other operations including reduction of fractures and repair of tissues after serious injuries. I seemed to have a natural ability for surgery that was encouraged by my senior surgeons. I loved the work and loved being able to make my patients better by interesting but relatively simple operative procedures. Regardless of the hours of work, RMO salaries in those days were very low. I remember receiving my first week's pay cheque. It was five pounds, just the price of a sports jacket, a luxury that I had long wanted to buy, so I spent the whole of my first week's pay on one green tweed sports jacket.

My friend and senior RMO, Toby Bowering, who was responsible for our rostering and supervision, was also a very good teacher. The hospital's medical superintendent was virtually retired and played little part in the running of the hospital, leaving everything of clinical significance to Toby. Many years later Toby became Foundation Professor of Paediatric Surgery at Sydney's second medical school at the University of New South Wales, which was established about ten years after I graduated.

A happy event in my first year as an RMO was to get a holiday job as ship's surgeon in the *Wanganella*, a passenger ship that travelled regularly between Sydney and Wellington, New Zealand. Sydney Hospital and the Royal South Sydney Hospital had a contract with the shipping company to supply the mandatory doctor for each trip and of course there was always a long list of RMO applicants. I was one of the lucky ones. My first cruise was uneventful as far as medical work was concerned but very interesting and a lot of fun socially. It was that cruise that confirmed my ambition to work some day as a ship's surgeon.

After my year at the Royal South Sydney Hospital I wanted a position like Toby Bowering's as senior RMO in a smallish hospital, similar to the Royal South Sydney where I could play a role as a teacher and have more clinical responsibility than I would have in a major teaching hospital. I applied for and was appointed Senior RMO in the Western Suburbs Hospital. This was a very happy appointment for me as the hospital was near my mother's family home in Croydon. My Aunt Elsie had been a nurse there, and it was the only hospital in which I had been an in-patient. At the age of seven I had had my tonsils and adenoids removed there by a Dr Waddington who was still on the surgical staff. I still remember being given an open-ether anaesthetic for that childhood operation.

When I started work there, the medical superintendent, Dr Bill Doherty, was very different to the superintendent of the Royal South Sydney Hospital. He was a young man and a teaching dynamo. He demanded perfection in medical treatment but was always available for advice or help. Bill was also a competent surgeon, which could have been a problem for me as we both wanted to do as much surgery as possible. Fortunately our three junior RMO colleagues had little interest in surgery so to a large extent Bill and I divided most of the emergencies between us, only calling in a consultant for potentially difficult cases.

The three RMOs were Keith Guy, who was most interested in general medicine, Paul Lush and John Sturrock, both of whom later trained as specialists in psychiatry. The bonds of friendship became very strong, as we were all working long hours and were part of a mutually dependent group with a shared objective of giving the best care possible to our patients. We five hospital resident staff members all remained lifelong close friends. The requirement to live in the hospital's staff quarters, with only every second weekend off-duty, gave us excellent training and further strengthened our friendships. This arrangement also established a warmth and compassion between me and my patients that became a lifelong practice, as I am sure it did for most of my colleagues of that vintage. The small salaries we received were a bonus, not a precondition of employment, a situation I am sorry to say seems to have changed over more recent years.

As young, red-blooded, heterosexual Australian males we sometimes developed close friendships with the nursing staff. This occasionally led to complications. After one special date which involved breaking the strict nurses' curfew I remember trying to find an open window to the nurses' quarters for my companion to enter and upon being caught suffering a severe reprimand.

My younger brother, Bruce, occasionally came to visit me at the hospital. On one of these visits he was most impressed when he spotted a very attractive nurse, Thelma Jones, whom he subsequently started dating. Thelma must also have been impressed with Bruce: she has been my sister-in-law for over fifty years.

Chapter Two

Broader Horizons

Assistant Surgeon on the *Orontes*

After my year as senior RMO at Western Suburbs Hospital I knew I had to be a surgeon. In 1952 the best training in surgery was in England or Scotland; somehow I had to arrange to get there by ship. I had no means of paying my way as a passenger so towards the end of my year at the hospital I began to enquire at every shipping company for a way to work my way to England. I am pleased to acknowledge the opportunities the shipping lines, especially the Orient Line and the P&O Line, provided for travel to the UK in those days. Air travel was in its infancy and was expensive. Travelling by ship was usually too expensive for young medical graduates but these shipping companies provided free travel in return for working as assistant surgeon to and from the UK. There was always a waiting list of young Australian doctors to get an appointment so the shipping companies allocated the positions to the young doctors they considered would be most likely to benefit from overseas experience. Similarly they allocated positions of assistant surgeon on a return voyage to Australia to doctors who had acquired specialist qualifications and experience that were most needed in Australia.

I must have driven the shipping companies mad. At every enquiry I was told there were no foreseeable vacancies and to try again in three months. Every couple of weeks I would ask again but was repeatedly told to try again in two or three months. Eventually I had a call from the Australian manager of the Orient Shipping Company to tell me that an assistant surgeon on their 20,000-ton passenger ship, *Orontes*, had taken ill and if I was prepared to leave in ten days I could take his place. That was in March 1953.

I had been filling in time by getting experience in general practice as a locum for a friend and Western Suburbs Hospital visiting physician, Dr Les Dunlop, in Ashfield. He happily wished me well, Mum helped me convert a navy-blue suit into a ship surgeon's uniform, and I set sail for England on the *Orontes*. Some years later I discovered that the ship that brought my Dad home from the war about 34 years before was also named the *Orontes*. Owned by the same shipping company, the Orient Line, my ship was a relatively new replacement for the old *Orontes*.

I thoroughly enjoyed life as a big ocean liner's assistant surgeon for the six weeks it took to sail to England. I found it much more fun than I believe I would have if I had been travelling as a passenger, although it was a fairly busy life. People became seasick, ate too much and drank too much, became sunburnt by the swimming pool in the tropical sun, and there were some accidents – for instance a couple of elderly ladies received broken wrists after falls due to the rolling of the ship.

I was also expected to be the ship's dentist. We had a dentist's handbook and a container of dental instruments in our surgery and I remember when asked by a member of crew to extract a rotting, aching tooth I had to look up the handbook to find what particular pliers were recommended. Under local anaesthetic I removed the tooth successfully but my hospital assistant advised me that it was always important to check that the roots of any extracted tooth had been removed entirely. He told me that a previous ship's doctor had kept a cricket score card in the surgery, a tooth extracted in one piece was scored as one run and a root left in was a wicket down. So, as it happened I was 1 for 0.

Along the way, the *Orontes* stopped at a number of ports to put down or pick up passengers and replenish supplies. These stops included Melbourne, Adelaide, Fremantle (Perth), Colombo, Aden, Suez, Port Said, Naples and Gibraltar, before we finally docked at Tilbury, England. At these port stops, the passengers would leave the ship for a day trip and often developed gastric problems from the unusual food that they had eaten. And if a child presented with a rash or some other infectious disease it would usually affect other children on the ship. Nevertheless, the ship had a reasonable hospital, two experienced nurses and a general assistant for the hospital.

The role of assistant surgeon came with many privileges, including wearing an officer's uniform with one and a half-gold stripes, ready access to sporting, games and dance facilities and a head of table position in the dining room. As an Australian, I was expected to play deck-cricket and deck tennis, and was usually asked to captain one of the cricket teams. There were many pretty girls on the ship and some enjoyed the assistant surgeon's company when time permitted by day or by night. One young lady in particular became quite special to me. We spent the day together in Colombo, Aden, Naples and Gibraltar, seeing the sights.

Unhappily after arrival in England we had only a few days seeing some of the attractions of London together before she was booked to return to her work and her family in New York.

The Torbay Hospital, Torquay

Having arrived in London without any arrangements for a place to work I decided that although I wanted a job in surgery I might settle in better if I could find employment out of the capital. I looked up job advertisements in the British Medical Journal and bought a tourist guidebook to help me select a pleasant location. I eventually found a vacancy for a senior RMO in surgery at Torbay Hospital in Torquay on the south coast of Devon, a town since made famous by the TV comedy series 'Faulty Towers'.

I applied for and was immediately appointed RMO. It was a good place to live and work. The surgical staff were very competent and delightful people to work with. As in Australia in those days the term 'resident medical officer' meant exactly that. Junior, senior and registrar medical officers were required to live in the hospital quarters for doctors and were required to be available for the care of their patients day and night with official time off only every second weekend. The patients, medical and nursing staff, were very unpretentious and likeable people, and considered an Australian doctor to be something of a novelty. Unlike in Australia there was still rationing of clothes and petrol in force following World War II. World war memories were still so vivid that people in Britain were still full of gratitude for the support given in so many ways by Australians during the war years.

My six months at Torbay hospital were a delightful introduction to England from all points of view, including receiving good training and experience in surgery. It was the time of the coronation of Queen Elizabeth II and Australian loyalty and participation in Empire events and traditions was widely appreciated.

On my first weekend covering emergency and casualty duties at Torbay there was a phone call from a nearby racetrack. An important jockey had fallen off his horse and broken his leg. The jockey was in fact Freddie Winter, Britain's leading jockey at that time. The racing officials said that they were bringing Mr Winter to the hospital and asked me to call our most senior orthopaedic surgeon to be prepared to give immediate attention, but try as I did I could not find an available orthopod.

When Mr Winter arrived he was surrounded by a plethora of concerned pinstriped, bowler-hatted officials who again demanded the services of the hospital's most senior orthopaedic surgeon. I had to explain that being a holiday weekend the gentleman was apparently sailing his boat on Torbay Harbour. The officials then asked me to arrange transport to London and for me to alert London's top orthopaedic surgeon. I examined the broken leg, which had bone poking out through the skin (a compound fracture). Then I insisted on speaking to the patient alone and dismissed the troubled officials. Freddie Winter was a very pleasant and understanding man and when I advised him that this was an emergency situation and that at the very least the wound had to be washed and closed to prevent serious infection, he readily agreed. This I did under local anaesthesia because there was no anaesthetist readily available. I cleaned and closed the wound. The fracture was in a good position so I applied a plaster and Freddie was admitted to a private room in the hospital under the care of the senior orthopaedic surgeon who eventually arranged for him to be transferred to the London Clinic under the care of Sir Reginald Watson-Jones, Britain's best-known orthopaedic surgeon and author of the most accepted textbook of orthopaedic surgery.

Before leaving Torbay hospital Freddie thanked me for my care and advised me to 'back Nikemu the following Tuesday'. I of course did not know anything about Nikemu nor did I have any idea where to find a bookmaker. I promptly forgot Freddie's tip but some days later I remembered to look up the race results. Of course Nikemu had easily won a race somewhere on Tuesday at 4 to 1.

But that wasn't the only 'adventure' I had at Torbay hospital. Late one night I was phoned by an angry Irish doctor who had been dissatisfied with something that someone at the hospital had done or not done. When he let out a torrent of abuse in language I still don't use I said to him 'You wouldn't be game to say that to me in person'.

'Wouldn't I? Just wait and see, I'll be there in a few minutes', he thundered.

True to his word he knocked on the hospital door moments later. He was a fairly thickset man in an obvious rage, possibly heightened by alcohol. He demanded we settle our differences by fisticuffs on the hospital lawn. I told him that it would be silly for grown men, much less doctors, to fight and, in any case, I was taller than he was and I had done a little boxing as a student. I then asked some nearby nurses to be my witnesses that I was not going to hit this man unless he hit me first. He subsequently landed a few punches on me so I opened up and floored him with one lucky punch to the jaw. I thought for a moment that I had killed him but he soon picked himself up and got into his car. I asked him not to leave because the nurses had called the local police, but he drove off. When the police arrived I told them what had happened but suggested they go to his home to be sure that he had arrived safely. They told me later that although he had seemed sorry for himself he had arrived home safely and didn't appear to have been seriously injured.

The news of this fracas quickly got around the hospital and I was summoned to appear before a committee comprising the senior surgeon, senior physician, hospital board chairman, hospital secretary and matron, to explain myself. Before the meeting, each one of the committee members took me aside and thanked me for giving this troublesome doctor a dose of his own medicine which he apparently had long deserved. Each suggested that when I was before the committee I should tell my story and apologise for anything I had done wrong and all would be forgiven and forgotten.

Officially, all went smoothly, but the rumour mill went into overdrive. A few days later the senior orthopaedic surgeon took me aside and asked me if I knew anything about a recent disturbance in the hospital. He said, 'I believe there was some fighting with an Irish doctor and I can only ask you because I know you would not have been in it'. He suggested one or two names of staff he thought were likely to be aggressive and asked did I know who was involved. When I confessed, he said 'So that's how Dr —— got his injuries. I have just treated him for a fractured ankle and a fractured jaw but he told me it had just been an accident, he had slipped on some wet leaves.' Apparently I had fractured his jaw and he had fractured his ankle when he fell. An amusing consequence of that event was that I was invited by the hospital's pathologist, who happened also to be the president of the local boxing club, to join his club. I declined, but he and I became good friends.

I loved Torquay. I spent my first British Christmas there and thoroughly enjoyed it. As senior surgical resident I was expected to carve the Christmas turkey in each of the wards and a few days before leaving I had my first ever experience of snow, allegedly a rare event in Devon. I had felt very much at home in Devon and Cornwall and it came as no great surprise that I discovered many years later it was from this part of England my Stephens forefathers had lived before emigrating to Australia. But after a total of six happy months in Torquay I accepted a position at The London Metropolitan Hospital, for which I had applied some months before supported by the surgeons at Torbay. I was appointed senior resident medical officer (SRMO) to the famous London surgeon, Mr McNeil Love, who was co-author of the surgical textbook, 'Bailey and Love', that remains to this day the most widely used surgical text in Britain and in Australia. An offer for me to work as SRMO in his unit was too good to refuse.

The Metropolitan Hospital, London

So off to London I went in January 1954. I found my way to The Metropolitan Hospital in the East End and was warmly welcomed by all of the staff including a very competent registrar (trainee specialist) from South Africa, Percy Helman, who, some years later became Professor of surgery in Capetown. Percy introduced me to another 'colonial' RMO, who was from the West Indies. In spite of apartheid in South Africa at that time the atmosphere in the hospital was such that this very fair South African and very black

West Indian became very good friends. As in Torquay, living in the hospital to be available for patients under my care day and night was part of the 'RMO' requirement. However this hospital in London's east-end had a difference. Not only was I shown around the hospital I was also introduced to the pub across the road as though it was an integral part of the hospital. It was a common meeting place for hospital staff. Something I had never heard of before, or since, was that the pub was listed in the hospital's telephone directory and had a direct connection to the hospital's telephone system. Being a virtual non-drinker, I was surprised by this level of intimacy between hostelry and hospital but grew to love the system where the hospital staff could meet together and with East-End residents to discuss everything from medical matters to politics and sport (especially cricket, tennis or rugby when I was there).

Naturally I was held responsible for everything Australian sportspeople had done or had failed to do. Sometimes this was to my distinct advantage; on one occasion I won a beautiful pullover in a bet on the outcome of a cricket match between England and Australia. This was one of the wonderfully competitive 1954–1955 'Ashes' series in which two best friends and everyone's favourite cricketers were playing: Keith Miller for Australia and Dennis Compton for England. I was lucky because my bet was that in the first innings Keith Miller would make more runs than Dennis Compton. In fact Compton made only 4 runs in the first innings and Miller made only 7. Luckily for me there were no bets on the second innings in which Compton made more than Miller and England went on to win the test and the series thanks to their famous fast bowler, 'Typhoon' Tyson.

The pub had a congenial, friendly atmosphere, as is common in English pubs, and I particularly liked the beer that had such a low alcohol content it could be sipped all night without noticeably affecting either myself or my friends and colleagues. I don't think I ever saw anyone badly affected by alcohol but I did meet real Londoners there. Delightful people though they were I was sometimes amazed by their insularity. On one occasion, on hearing that I came from Sydney, a man asked:

'Do you happen to know Claude Vincent'.

'I know some people called Vincent but I don't remember any

Claude Vincent. Is he a doctor?'

'No he is an engineer I think'.

'Was he at Sydney University?'

'No, I think he was at Capetown University. He lives in Capetown'.

'But, Capetown is in South Africa'.

'I know but it's all down that way isn't it, I thought you might know him'.

The first time I was scheduled to assist Mr McNeil Love in surgery was for a gallbladder operation. Percy Helman, Mr Love's registrar, warned me that there were two standard questions our boss would be likely to ask me about the gallbladder. The first would be 'What is the colour of a normal gallbladder'? The answer he wanted was 'slate-blue'. His second question would then be 'What does it pay to forget when you are doing a gallbladder operation'? The answer he wanted was, 'Any concept of normal anatomy'. This is because the anatomy of the gallbladder ducts and arteries is very variable.

Sure enough, after we had started, Mr Love asked, 'Stephens my boy, what is the colour of the normal gall bladder?' Not wanting to appear too obviously primed for the question I hesitated and answered, 'Well it's a greenish-bluish colour, sir, not quite green but not quite blue. I suppose it is more of a slate-blue colour'.

'Very good' he said.

A little while later he asked, 'Stephens, my boy, what does it pay to forget when doing a gallbladder operation?' Again I hesitated for a while so that my access to inside information would not be obvious: 'Well, sir, the anatomy in the gallbladder region is very variable. The artery is sometimes in front of the duct, sometimes behind it, sometimes there are two arteries, and sometimes there is no duct at all. I suppose it pays to forget any concept of normal anatomy sir'. Not to be fooled, the great man smiled at me and said: 'Stephens, they have been priming you for this, haven't they?' We got on famously after that.

One of my duties at 'The Met' was to take my turn in care of the casualty and emergency department. On one of my mornings off, I had arranged to take an attractive nurse to see Ken Rosewall play at Wimbledon, but I was called urgently to the emergency department where a man had run amok and punched a rather timid wardsman in the face. I was called because the casualty doctor on duty was a small woman and I happened to be the biggest doctor on the staff. When I saw the man I asked him if he had hit the wardsman. He answered with abuse that would make a wharfie blush. I pointed to him and said: 'Get out you bastard, get out'.

At first he turned to go then he hesitated and turned back.

'Now get out or I'll throw you out,' I said.

Again he started to leave, but then he turned to me and said meekly: 'Doctor you just don't understand, I have come here for treatment because I go around hitting people'. I was lost for words. I called the emergency psychiatric service and explained to my girlfriend that I needed to stay and watch the man until the service had arrived. Unfortunately I had to wait all day and it was too late to go to the tennis.

We still had tickets to see the men's singles final later on when Ken Rosewall played an Egyptian named Drobny and lost. That was one occasion when I was angry with the English. With the exception of my English companion who barracked with me for Rosewall, the crowd clearly supported Drobny. I felt this crowd at the centre of our British Empire had been disloyal to Australia and particularly to Ken Rosewall who was not only a great young tennis player, but also a loyal citizen of the empire and a great ambassador for his country. My tennis companion and I became very good friends but we eventually went our separate ways and married other people.

One enjoyable feature of being at The Met was easy the access to London's wonderful live theatre district. The theatres of London were, and still are, magical. I saw many shows during my time there including *The Boy-Friend*, *Kismet*, *Oklahoma*, *Salad Days*, *Pal Joey* and *The King and I*. I was generally accompanied by an amicable nurse companion who was happy to sit with me in the cheapest possible 'two bob' seats 'in the gods' which were all I could afford.

There was an annual tradition at The Met for the resident medical staff to pay a visit to one of London's old music halls, the Collins Music Hall, close by in the East End. The famous high quality theatres are in the more posh West End, but the Collins was among the few cheap old-fashioned fun burlesque/vaudeville theatres that remained in the East End. My colleagues told me that it was usual to have some invited audience participation in some of the sketches and dances and that on one occasion an RMO had volunteered to go onto the stage. While on stage he had invited some of the dancing-girls back to the hospital for a party. A whole row of seats was booked for our 1954 visit but when we arrived my friends insisted that I must sit on the end of the row. When there was a call for a male to volunteer to join the dancing-girls on stage, my colleagues, more-or-less pushed me onto the stage with instructions to invite the dancing-girls back for a party. Up close I could see why these 'girls' were working in burlesque theatre. They were very much past their prime and appeared to be at least 20 or 30 years older than any of us. I don't think my mates ever quite forgave me for not inviting them back to our party.

I was also called as a witness at the Old Bailey in cases involving trauma or violence to patients whom I had treated in The Met. I would be called under threat of a fine if I did not appear but would usually sit there for hours without being called. But I was paid an attendance fee and there was a great variety of criminal trials, mostly involving violence. I quite enjoyed these visits to the Old Bailey. To me they exposed a way of life previously unknown to me. I realised how fortunate I had been to have had such a protected life with such a loving family in my Kurmond childhood.

A very special memory for me was to have a seat in the House of Commons in November 1954 on the day on which Winston Churchill thanked the members of parliament for honouring him on his 80th birthday.

After my year in the London Metropolitan Hospital I decided that it was time I studied seriously for my postgraduate surgical qualification, a Royal College of Surgeons fellowship.

The Primary Surgical Fellowship examination

The Royal Colleges of Surgeons of England, Edinburgh, Glasgow, and Ireland as well as Australasia all have a two-part (two stage) examination for admission to fellowship. The results of the examinations in the first stage (consisting of anatomy, physiology and other basic sciences) are mutually acceptable to all colleges. If the candidate has passed the primary examination of any one college that pass is accepted by all of the colleges but the results in the second stage examinations are not mutually acceptable. They are discrete to the examining college so that to be awarded the Fellowship of the Royal College of Surgeons of England (FRCS), for example, the examination must be passed in London. The same applies for each of the other colleges. Each college stands on some assumed dignity of believing that it has a higher standard than the other colleges and therefore only people who pass their particular examination are worthy of their fellowship diploma. To my way of thinking this is self-aggrandising nonsense. Nevertheless, with certain exceptions, it still stands and gives the college officials something to do, a lot of ceremony and a strong belief in their own self-importance.

It was convenient for me to study for the primary examination at The Royal College of Surgeons of England. Although the examinations were similar, this college provided the best courses and best study facilities, especially for the primary fellowship examination.

I arranged to live in London House, a most convenient, comfortable and inexpensive college in Russel Square, provided especially for overseas postgraduate students to attend courses of study. Over the years many Australians, New Zealanders, Canadians, Indians and South Africans have been well served by this facility near the heart of London. I was lucky enough to be accepted onto the primary fellowship course in London, which I attended for six months. The Royal College of Surgeons examinations are renowned for being very tough exams. It is necessary to pass all subjects together but few people pass all subjects at the first attempt and some make many attempts.

In London one candidate, Simon R, had attempted the primary examination several times. Simon was fronting up for his sixth attempt but happened to be allocated to a kindly examiner who boasted that he always liked to start by asking a question that the candidate could answer comfortably. This was to help the candidate relax. When Simon sat before the examiner the examiner said, 'Now please sit down and be comfortable. Your face is familiar, have we met before?'

Simon replied, 'Yes sir we have met before, at this examination last year'.

The examiner apologised, 'I'm so sorry, I did not mean to

embarrass you, but just tell me what was the first question I asked you then?'

Simon answered, 'Where have we met before, sir'!

Another examiner often asked candidates about variations of the anatomy of the gall bladder and the bile ducts. If the candidate answered all questions well he then sometimes asked, 'What animal does not have a gall bladder'? The answer he expected was 'the horse'. On one occasion when the candidate had given correct answers to all questions about the variations of anatomy of the gall bladder and bile ducts, the examiner asked the candidate 'What animal does not have a gall bladder'? The candidate was an Australian who, quick as a flash, answered 'The kangaroo, sir'. The examiner had no idea about kangaroos' gall bladders so he asked the candidate 'What about the horse?' The candidate stood his ground and retorted 'What about the kangaroo, sir'!

(An unusual collection of animals do not have a gallbladder, but the kangaroo is not one of them. Animals that do not have a gall bladder are quite a diverse group, the horse, the llama, the whale, the rat and the pigeon.)

I was expected to do well and possibly take the prize for anatomy but I failed the anatomy examination. I found that embarrassing as I had unofficially been tutoring some fellow students in anatomy. Professor Ray Last, the renowned Professor of anatomy, who unknown to me at the time happened to be an Australian, called me into his office and invited me to apply for a job as 'prosector in anatomy', a teaching position.

Naturally I applied for this position and was appointed in the Autumn of 1954. I officially became a teacher in anatomy at the Royal College of Surgeons in London and lived inexpensively in the college hostel. There I studied with and tutored other friends. I passed the examination at my second attempt.

At the Royal College of Surgeons in London I also studied with a number of Australians and I became a close friend of Dr Geoffrey Cutler whose older brother, Sir Roden Cutler VC, was later to become Governor of New South Wales. I have since learned that Geoff and his brother had also been students at Sydney High School a few years before I enrolled at the school. Geoff and I decided to apply for a three month advanced surgical training course at

St Thomas's Hospital London. Both our applications were successful so we worked and studied closely together for the next three months

It was in a class at St Thomas's that one of the teachers, Dr Shuttleworth, said: 'Cancer is our greatest unsolved health problem; I suggest that in your future practices you keep in mind that something you may notice as an apparently unrelated incident may give you a clue about cause or treatment of cancer, or at least a new insight into cancer that has not before been considered.' This thoughtful message made a lasting impression upon me and from then on I looked at things differently. I began to take a special interest in cancer and the need to think about improving the knowledge and treatment of the disease. I decided that after my training in general surgery was completed I would concentrate on seeking better methods of cancer treatment.

Both Geoff and I completed the St Thomas's surgical course and Geoff presented himself and passed the next final FRCS examination. However, I felt that I needed more practical surgical experience – and I certainly needed more money in the bank before presenting for the final FRCS examination.

St Leonard's Hospital, London

I enquired at St Leonard's Hospital in Kingsland Road, the same road as The Met. St Leonard's needed a locum registrar for three months to work with a surgeon with a knighthood and I felt lucky to be appointed almost immediately. Although my chief at that hospital was a knight of the realm and was treated with the deference often shown to a Master surgeon, from my observations I did not think he had a high level of surgical expertise. I later learnt he had an inherited his knighthood. Years later near the end of my professional life I realised that this man's circumstances were not exceptional. Not only are knighthoods sometimes inherited but the greatest accolades in surgery, including knighthoods, are sometimes bestowed on those who play professional politics well. Surgeons I have known who spend their time practising the highest standards of care, or researching better ways of care, have often missed out on this sort of recognition for want of political know-how.

There was an added attraction for the younger staff at St Leonard's: ease of illicit access between the resident doctor's quarters and the nurses' home. The hospital was built in three sections. The centre was the large administration and patient care block. On one side was the resident doctors quarters, and on the other side, the nurses home. Theoretically these were three separate buildings but somehow they had deep basements connected by tunnels. It was as though the hospital had been built on ancient dungeons. It was interesting to see the flow of traffic at night from the doctors' quarters to the nurses' home and vice-versa.

Assistant Surgeon on the *Otranto*

I had spent two years in England by then and at that time it was a requirement that any Commonwealth male resident of the United Kingdom of my age who had not done national service in his country of origin was required to do British national service. Most students were granted exemption from this requirement, but when I was given the choice of serving in the British Army, Navy, or Air Force I was also told of the sudden need for an assistant surgeon in a passenger/migrant merchant ship and that this would satisfy the requirements.

The position was in the Orient Company passenger liner *Otranto* which was sailing to Australia. It was a perfect opportunity for me to visit my family in Australia whom I missed very much. Although I had written home regularly to share my adventures and experiences with them, I looked forward to being with them in person and to show them the movie films that I had taken in the different countries I had visited. I often regretted that my mother had never been able to travel abroad and my father had only ever had one overseas adventure – during the Great War – and that had ended badly for him. I signed up immediately.

The *Otranto* was a sister-ship to the *Orontes* and as with the *Orontes*, the tourist class passengers were almost all migrants to Australia. They were a very nice group of friendly, somewhat excited people who were full of hope and ambition. The ship took the same route to and from Sydney as I had experienced on the *Orontes*. From Tilbury Docks (England) we were to stop at Gibraltar, Naples, Navarino Bay (in Greece), Port Said, Suez, Aden, Colombo, Perth, Adelaide, Melbourne and finally Sydney. The route was familiar but all the staff were new to me.

The senior surgeon, Paddy Morrissey, a Dubliner, was one of the original Irish fun doctors with a larrikin sense of humour. He was a good doctor and took his work seriously but that didn't stop him enjoying life at sea and especially enjoying the company of glamorous members of the opposite sex whether they were passengers or crew. In fact, some years later when his philandering days were over, Paddy eventually married a member of the ship's company whose job was to care for children aboard ship. They eventually settled in London where Paddy established a general practice.

The most exciting medical event on the voyage to Sydney was that a woman member of the crew developed 'an acute abdomen' in the middle of the Indian Ocean. She was in considerable pain, vomiting, feverish and very tender in the right side of her abdomen. Paddy and I both thought she had a very acute appendicitis, possibly a ruptured appendix, and needed immediate surgery. As Paddy had little experience in surgery, he agreed to give the anaesthetic while I operated, assisted by our two nurses. We set up an operating room, the ship's captain changed course to avoid as much rolling of the ship as possible, and Paddy gave a good old-fashioned 'open ether' anaesthetic. I then made an incision on the right side of the lady's abdomen to find – not an acute appendix – but an acutely inflamed, pus-filled, gallbladder, possibly about to rupture. I removed it, and all went well with the operation.

In those days large long-distance passenger ships had hospitals and a hospital attendant. The *Otranto* had a 4 bed hospital that often had one or two patients in it. There was also a mandatory supply of medications and some equipment, but many of the medications would have been right at home in my mother's medical chest of many years previously, useful only to past generations of ships' medical practitioners. After her operation we cared for our patient in the hospital but soon discovered intravenous fluids were in short supply. We had only one bottle (one litre) of normal saline and two bottles of dextrose/saline, which we duly administered and the patient did well. When we berthed at Fremantle we insisted, against her wishes, that she be admitted to hospital in Perth for a few days and we picked her up again on our return voyage.

Arriving in Sydney was wonderful. Any Sydneysider who has been away for a couple of years will relate to the butterflies I felt in my tummy as we sailed up that beautiful harbour and saw the harbour bridge at dawn. My parents and some of my brothers and sisters were there to greet me and I had the pleasure of showing them over the ship. I had a wonderful week in Sydney with family and friends and I even paid a visit to see my old home in Kurmond where I was surprised to see how so much had changed in the district.

On our return voyage a most exciting event happened when we were passing through the Suez Canal. Stowaways of all ages can be found in most unusual places but this one was still in his mother's uterus. A woman, already the mother of five, was about 8 months pregnant and threatened to come into early labour. She did not want to be put into hospital in Egypt so Paddy and I agreed to care for her on-board ship. The threatening evidence of delivery came and went for a few days but then suddenly she went into labour when we were in the middle of the Mediterranean Sea. Paddy allowed me to deliver the baby while he sedated the mum. All went well and a bonnie baby boy of about 6 pounds (2.7 kilos) was delivered.

Naturally it is impossible to keep such events confidential in the close confines of a ship that is carrying more than 2000 people. After the birth of a healthy baby boy was announced parties broke out all over the ship. Apparently there were many sweepstakes on the sex and weight of the baby, and the latitude and longitude of the place of delivery. From each party a bottle of champagne was sent down to the mother and father. The baby breast-fed readily and progressed well until with only a few days travel to go, he refused to feed and became restless and upset. Nothing we did seemed to help until I realised that the mother was no longer getting bottles of champagne and consequently her baby was not getting a second-hand supply of champagne in his breast milk.

We arranged for the mum to be supplied with a glass of stout before each feed and the baby again drank readily and slept well. He just needed a little alcohol. Naturally we weaned both mother and baby off alcohol as soon as we could so that by the time we reached our final destination he slept well without it in his breast milk and we heard some years later that he had grown into a happy, healthy little boy.

Following the birth the ship's captain and an Anglican minister, who happened to be a passenger, arranged to have the baby christened at sea. Paddy and I were asked to be Godparents and to have the baby named after us. Unhappily the parents were not excited at having their baby named either Fred or Oscar (a little disappointment that continues whenever my children choose a name for my grandsons), so they made a compromise and their son was named Stephen Patrick.

Whilst all this was happening Paddy and I noticed two very attractive young ladies boarding the ship with their parents in Naples, so we arranged to take them ashore at Gibraltar and had a lovely day.

Happily, Paddy took a greater interest in the 21-year-old while I fancied the taller 19-year-old. During the last days of the voyage Paddy invited the girls to have a week's holiday with us in Ireland. The girls explained that this would require their parents' approval. Somehow Paddy convinced the girls' parents that we would be spending the holiday with his dear old mother who would take good care of them. They eventually consented and Paddy arranged to travel immediately to Dublin to make arrangements, and for me to take the girls a couple of days later by train to Wales and then by ferry to Dublin.

All went to plan but after meeting us in Dublin Paddy took us to a hotel. He had made two double-bed room bookings, one for him and the older sister; and the other for me and the younger sister. I told Paddy that I didn't have that sort of relationship with the girl and that I also thought she would probably object.

'What else do you think they would be expecting on a holiday with us in Ireland', Paddy replied. But I was right. The sisters insisted on sharing one of the rooms together and Paddy and I were dismissed to the second bedroom. As there was only one double bed in each room Paddy and I had to share a bed. It was not very pleasant for either of us. We were both uncomfortable and by the morning Paddy was so angry that 'the girls had led us on' he refused to have anything to do with them for the rest of the holiday.

When I returned to London I was summoned to the Orient Line head office where I was advised that Paddy was to be promoted to Senior Surgeon on one of the company's bigger and newer ships. I was therefore offered his former post as Senior Surgeon on the *Otranto*. I accepted because it meant being able to visit Australia again.

Senior Surgeon on the *Otranto*

A Senior Surgeon's Role carried extra responsibilities. These included checking that all necessary medical supplies were on board and preparing a mandatory list of medications. It also included completing accurate medical records of all passengers and crew; 'clearing the ship' at every port (which meant satisfying authorities that we weren't carrying anyone with a dangerous infectious disease), and conducting daily spot inspections with the captain to check the cleanliness and upkeep of all rooms and facilities. At 11 am each day a different part of the ship was chosen for inspection.

The role had distinct advantages including more pay, the right to charge a fee for treatment of first-class passengers, consigning mundane tasks to the assistant surgeon, and wearing three gold stripes on my uniforms. It also gave me free access to any part of the ship and to head a dining room table next to the captain's with the right to choose any of the passengers as table companions. To me this was a particularly useful privilege. As assistant surgeon I would take note of the most appealing passengers boarding at each port and for a small consideration the chief steward would allocate a place for them at my table – that is unless the captain or some other senior officer saw them first. As Senior Surgeon I had first choice.

Whenever he could, the captain loved to have me partner him on any golf courses in ports along the way. I suspect this was because he had at last found a golfer with less golfing talent than he had himself. He won most of our matches. Actually, when in port I preferred escorting one of the many pretty female passengers to playing golf with the captain – but unfortunately orders were orders.

In my three journeys as Senior Surgeon between England and Australia my Assistant Surgeons all gained specialist qualifications and later became highly distinguished specialists in Australia. Amongst those who returned with me to Australia were Jim Lance who became a very distinguished Professor of Neurology at The University of New South Wales, John Segelov who became a highly skilled Neurosurgeon at the Royal Prince Alfred Hospital in Sydney and Gavan Carroll who was appointed specialist visiting-anaesthetist at the Mater Hospital in Brisbane. Alex Gorshenin who travelled with me to England gained specialist qualifications in Ear Nose and Throat Surgery in England and later returned to a specialist practice in Queensland. Alex later married TV star Lorrae Desmond.

My first journey to Australia as Senior Surgeon was uneventful but on the return journey there was considerable drama. A member of the crew, a bedroom steward, jumped overboard. Some lifebelts were thrown overboard and the captain turned the ship around to search for the man in the dark in the middle of the Indian Ocean. A search was made for two or three hours but no trace could be found in the rolling sea. Prayers were said and the ship continued its voyage to the next port, Aden. An enquiry revealed that the steward had had a row with his boyfriend and decided to end it all.

Ships took six weeks to travel between Australia and England but they always stopped for about 24 hours in each of the major ports along the way. At each port some passengers would disembark and others would embark. We would also take on new supplies of food as well as fuel for the ship. It was interesting to note changes in our dining-room menus after we had stopped at certain ports; for example after Colombo we always had new supplies of tropical fruits and fresh vegetables.

While at sea it was quite common to receive a call to ask for medical advice from other ships that didn't carry a doctor. I would have to ask about the symptoms of any sick person and enquire about what medications or facilities were available on board and then give advice as best I could. It was rather like the radio advice given by Australia's Flying Doctors, and in most cases the problem was solved or at least could be palliated until the ship involved reached its next port.

On my second outward-bound voyage as Senior Surgeon we had a quite serious drama. Somewhere in the Red Sea the captain received a call from an Italian cargo ship asking for medical help. A crewman had had his arm mangled in some machinery and his ship had no doctor. Our two ships were manoeuvred close to one another and in the middle of the night I was lowered in a lifeboat to attend to the injured man. His arm was badly injured and he had lost some tissue (skin and muscle). I dressed the wound and took him back to our ship where we had much better facilities for his care. My assistant surgeon gave an anaesthetic and with the help of the nurses I repaired his arm as much as was possible. We arranged for him to be hospitalised in the next port which was Aden.

On the return voyage when we stopped at Naples a shipping official and a city official (the mayor I think) came to the ship and asked for me. They expressed gratitude for the care I had given to the injured Italian crewman some weeks before and put a car and driver at my disposal to take me on a tour of any part of Naples or the region that I wanted to see. So, with an attractive companion I had a great tour of Naples, including the buried city of Pompeii below the dominating volcano Mount Vesuvius.

After leaving Perth on the return leg of my last London-Sydney voyage there was another drama in the middle of the Indian Ocean. One of the crewmen was found apparently dead in his bath. Because of the importance of not upsetting the passengers such 'news' is always kept as quiet as possible. Arrangements were made with the captain and other officers for burial at sea. When all was ready for the burial with the Union Jack and a body bag at the ready I was summoned, as was legally required, to officially pronounce the death of the man.

I found a big fat man lying in an empty bathtub. The bathplug had been removed and all water had escaped. I looked at him and he truly appeared to be dead. He wasn't breathing, his eyes were closed and he didn't react to pain. He had neither a detectable pulse nor an audible heartbeat. To be sure he had expired I held a mirror in front of his nose and mouth and saw the faintest fogging on the mirror. Realising that he might be recoverable I applied artificial respiration and was gradually able to hear faint heart sounds and feel a pulse. Slowly he began to make movements and more slowly still he recovered. He had been 'dead drunk'. I still wonder if he ever realised how close he had come to being buried at sea.

On my last outward-bound voyage to Sydney I had a happy romance that was quite different from my other shipboard romances. After a holiday in Europe Deborah, blonde and beautiful, was returning home to Perth. The tired old blonde jokes did not apply to Debbie. She was level-headed and smart. We became engaged and she came to Sydney to meet my family. My family were delighted that I had at last shown signs of settling down and they were very pleased that my intended was such a nice young woman. I arranged for her to return to England with me on our next return voyage.

Debbie joined our ship in Perth. We had a lot of fun on the voyage, including a memorable stop off in Egypt. Our sightseeing included seeing the pyramids and the Sphinx. I was reminded that this was the place where in 1915, as a young soldier, my Dad had completed his training before, with his battalion, he was transferred to those awful battlefields in Northern France where he was so dreadfully injured.

Although Debbie and I enjoyed being together when we arrived back in England, we gradually drifted apart. In retrospect it was probably more my fault than Debbie's. I wasn't ready to settle down and within a few weeks I could not resist an invitation to travel to South America as the second part of my British National Service. We mutually agreed to break off our engagement.

Back on dry land – but not for long

After completing four round trips to Australia and therefore one year of national service I thought I would apply for exemption from the second year. I knew it would be granted and therefore I retired from the Orient Line with every intention of returning to serious study for the second part of a Fellowship examination in Surgery.

However, I knew that I needed further hospital and surgical experience so I applied for and was appointed to a surgical registrar locum position at the Nelson Hospital in Wimbledon for a month. Wimbledon had a special fascination for me because of its connection with tennis – a sport I had played and had been interested in since childhood, and of course the hospital had a tennis court so that now I can proudly boast that I have played tennis at Wimbledon.

Following my month at Wimbledon I decided to gain more general experience by working in obstetrics and gynaecology and I duly applied for and was appointed to a women's hospital, the All Saints Hospital in Stratham, Kent. Given all the joy and charm of bringing new babies into the world I had sometimes considered becoming an obstetrician. Although I loved delivering babies and sharing the happiness with the new mum and dad, I found that I actually spent most of my time doing routine obstetric clinics: feeling the tummies of normal pregnancies in women, checking blood pressures and urine, and discussing the choices of babies' names. The joy of delivering a healthy baby and presenting it to his or her parents is only a small part of the lengthy routine care of pregnancy which I found repetitious and without any medical challenge. Ultimately that was not professionally satisfying enough for me.

Whilst looking for a suitable locum surgical registrar training position I was asked if I would be interested in being surgeon with another shipping company six months hence. This temptation was too great to pass up and it also left me with six months to gain more hospital surgical experience, to undertake more study, and to save some money by working as a locum.

The *Highland Monarch* and South America

I accepted the enticing invitation to return to life as a ship's surgeon. My new ship was in the Royal Mail Line, a passenger and freight shipping company that operated between England and South America. I was offered the ship's Surgeon position on the *Highland Monarch* which started at Tilbury Docks and called at Vigo (Spain), Oporto (Portugal), The Canary Islands, Rio de Janeiro, Santos (Brazil), and Montevideo (Uruguay) before reaching its final destination in Buenos Aires, the capital of Argentina. The ship carried about 400 passengers as well as a cargo of manufactured goods. The stopover in Buenos Aires was usually for three weeks after which it returned to England via the same ports of call.

On the return voyage to London the ship also carried about 400 passengers but the main cargoes were meat from Argentina and tropical fruits, mainly bananas, from Brazil. There was one very significant difference to being a doctor in the *Highland Monarch* compared to my previous shipboard service: there was no assistant surgeon and no nursing staff or hospital attendant. The job was a one-man medical team responsible for about 400 passengers and 200 crew.

Its rank, privileges and responsibilities were similar to Senior Surgeon on the *Otranto*.

The first trip was interesting. Alcohol is duty free and very cheap on ships and being only a very moderate drinker I had made a rule while working as Ship's Surgeon that I would never consume more than three alcoholic drinks a day: a vow not so easy to keep. After each watch those of the ship's officers who had finished work usually had a few drinks together to which they invited the ship's doctor unless he was busy. Passengers were also in the habit of having a drink or two with meals and at their frequent after dinner parties. The surgeon was usually invited to these as well. After my self-imposed total of three drinks in any one day I would ask for Coca Cola, orange juice, or some other soft drink. The stewards therefore began to call me 'The Coca Cola Doc'. One of them told me that the previous surgeon had a notice on his door saying: 'The surgeon will be sober for consultation between 3 and 4 pm on alternate Thursdays'. He added, 'Then the bugger never was!'

On my first trip to Argentina we were carrying two champion motor racing drivers, Peter Collins of England and Wolfgang von Trips of Germany (whom we nicknamed Taffy). Peter and Taffy were great company. They were travelling to Argentina to race in the Argentine Grand Prix and invited me to be their 'honorary doctor' at the racetracks. This role included parties (one at the great Juan Fangio's home) and lots of other socialising. (Juan Fangio was world champion in 1951 and every year from 1953 to 1957). All the racing drivers whom I knew drank very little alcohol, which suited me, and they had a large following of attractive females which also suited me.

In Buenos Aires we met up with a number of other top racing drivers including Stirling Moss and Mike Hawthorn of Britain; Jean Beria of France; and Harry Schell of the United States. They were all great rivals on the racetrack but great friends in their personal lives. I liked them all. Formula I racing was then very dangerous. Only one of these men survived to retirement and he, Stirling Moss, was so badly injured in a race crash that he was lucky to survive. All of the others, and several more I met, died racing, either officially, or in the case of Mike Hawthorn simply speeding on a country road.

When I first left the ship to see Buenos Aires, I was warned by the ship's officers that I would probably be stopped by some of President Peron's military police and that I would be asked for identification papers and possibly taken to a police station for questioning. I was assured that the way to avoid this was to have a supply of tins of cigarettes with me. One tin of 50 cigarettes would apparently negate their intention to detain me – and so it proved to be. I was subsequently stopped by two police with fixed bayonets and asked for identification papers. Instead of my papers I handed them a tin of cigarettes and was allowed to pass.

Lillian

Mike Hawthorn and I were in a coffee bar having a cup of coffee when we noticed two beautiful girls seated at a nearby table. We asked them to join us and after a little persuasion they did. Mike asked me in a whisper which girl most interested me. I had no hesitation in choosing the beautiful auburn-haired brunette whose name was Lillian. Mike, like me, was taller than 6 feet and was happy that I had made this choice, since his preference in women was tall willowy blondes – a perfect description of Lillian's friend. We double-dated them on one or two occasions and took them to the Grand Prix.

In spite of the casual meeting, Lillian was very reserved and somewhat shy. She was also very proper and in some ways reminded me of my mother. There was to be no 'hanky-panky' with Lillian but I was sure that I wanted to see her again and arranged to meet her the next time my ship was due to dock in Buenos Aires. She spoke perfect English, German and Spanish. Argentina is predominantly a Spanish-speaking country but also has a significant population of other European migrants especially from Britain, Ireland, and Germany. Lillian was educated in a tri-lingual school that had lessons in English in the mornings and German in the afternoons, but all other activities, including sport, were conducted in Spanish. I thought it was a brilliant idea and years later I unsuccessfully tried to find it replicated in Australia for my own children.

The devil made me do it

The next outward voyage was not very eventful except for two discoveries. The first was that I had learned that the compulsory medications carried in the ship's surgery in a number of brown bottles would never be used in contemporary medicine. Some I had heard about in lectures about the history of medicine and others had long ago been superseded by better medications.

The second discovery was that it was illegal to carry alcohol into Argentina. Consequently my fellow officers were always on the lookout for someone who could find them an occasional drink on board ship while the ship's bar was compulsorily locked in port. Considering these two facts, a practical solution came to mind. Good quality drinks, especially brandy and sherry, were readily available en route at low cost in the ports of Vigo in Spain, and Oporto in Portugal so I discarded the useless contents of the multiple brown bottles in the surgery and replaced them with brandy and sherry. This way hospitality could be offered to shipboard mates or other guests when the ship was docked in Buenos Aires. All I can say in my defence is: 'The devil made me do it.'

A wildcat at sea

The only drama that I remember on that voyage had to do with a cat that was found on board in the middle of the Atlantic Ocean. It is illegal to bring an unquarantined animal into any South American port. The captain pragmatically declared that this cat had to be thrown overboard. When I heard this I felt sorry for the cat and suggested instead that I should 'put it to sleep' medically before it was 'buried' at sea. The captain agreed, so I took the cat to the surgery and looked for the most humane way to euthanase it. I thought a big dose of morphine would be best so with a kindly Steward holding the cat I injected it with a large dose of morphine. The cat immediately let out a loud screech, spread its claws and ran wild. Nobody was prepared to risk life and limb attempting to catch the wild, yowling, savage beast that had previously been so gentle. I have since learnt that this reaction is typical for cats exposed to morphine. A day or two later when someone found the cat and was prepared to approach it I found another anaesthetic that did calm the cat and put it to sleep forever.

Brazilian liver injections

I became aware of a curious phenomenon on my very first voyage to South America which was repeated on subsequent voyages: passengers who joined the ship in Brazil sometimes came to my surgery with a small vial of clear liquid for their 'weekly liver injection'. Neither they, nor anyone else, could tell me exactly what these injections were or what they did except in every case they had been medically prescribed 'to tone-up the liver'. I protested with the first patient but she insisted that she had to have it under her doctor's orders. She then presented me with a letter from her doctor asking me to give this patient her necessary liver injection without any indication as to what it was or what it was supposed to do for her liver.

With some reluctance I gave this lady her injection very slowly but as it did not seem to have any effect I became less concerned when subsequent passengers consulted me with a similar request. I still don't know what those injections were for. I suspect the substance might merely have been distilled water prescribed to satisfy neurotic patients who insisted that something had to be done for them. Perhaps this was a forerunner to the 'liver cleansing diets' of later years which achieved huge popularity and media coverage despite an absence of evidence to show they did anyone any good.

Brands Hatch

In London in 1957 while waiting for my third departure for South America, I decided to go to the Brands Hatch motor races where I met Mike Hawthorn who was soon to become world champion. Mike and I were having a drink together commiserating over the racetrack death a few weeks earlier of our mutual friend Peter Collins when a man tapped me on the shoulder and asked if I was Dr Stephens. I said that I was and he asked if I remembered him. I told him that his face was familiar but I couldn't quite place him. 'I'm Jack Brabham,' he said, 'you treated my little boy Geoffrey when he broke his arm on the *Otranto* on our way to England'. Of course I remembered. Jack, later Sir Jack, was then the up-and-coming star of motor-racing and went on to become world champion three times: in 1959, 1960 and 1966. His son Geoffrey has since also become a champion driver. Tragically just a few weeks after this encounter, Mike Hawthorn was killed, not in a race, but on a country road in England. Apparently Mike was 'speed testing' his new Jaguar.

Dentistry at sea

On the outward-bound journey of my third voyage, there was an amusing experience with a member of the crew. This crewman attended my surgery on three occasions complaining of toothache. Although he had a mouthful of rotten teeth on each occasion, at his instigation and under his direction, I extracted one particular decayed tooth that he claimed was aching. One day the captain asked me if I had been extracting this man's teeth. When I acknowledged that I had, the captain laughed and said this crewman was in the habit of becoming drunk and disorderly and each time he was put on a charge he would claim that he had been drinking excessively to alleviate severe toothache. This story helped him to avoid each charge but had meant he had to have a tooth extracted on each occasion to prove his veracity. I have sometimes wondered how many teeth he was prepared to forfeit to avoid any penalty.

Apart from this episode the outward voyage was devoid of drama, but my stay in Buenos Aires and the return voyage were quite eventful. In Buenos Aires I naturally spent what time I could with Lillian. Although I was not allowed any closer contact than an occasional cuddle and kiss, Lillian did show enough interest to take me home to meet her mother. This was a big deal for both of us. Her mother was a very pleasant woman and apparently approved of me so without any formal engagement Lillian and I began to talk about getting married.

However, our plans had to be put on hold for a while because I was committed to returning to England with my ship, and I had also applied for a serious job in surgical training in Scotland's Royal Infirmary, Aberdeen. Lillian had also arranged to complete her education in an American university in New York. We therefore agreed to put our wedding plans on hold but to keep in regular touch by mail until we had both completed our commitments.

Do-it-yourself surgery

On the return voyage, in mid Atlantic, I was called to see two young crewmen both of whom had developed severe abdominal pain and vomiting. There was no doubt that both had very acute appendicitis and both needed to have appendectomies without delay. As I was the only medical officer on board I asked if there was a doctor among the passengers who could give an anaesthetic. The sole respondent was an elderly, retired Spanish doctor who said he had given many anaesthetics and would be prepared to act as anaesthetist. There were no proper facilities on board for conducting abdominal surgery however there were a few instruments, including a scalpel and forceps. There were also some needles and a small amount of suture material, a few bandages and simple wound dressings, but there were no surgical swabs, major dressing materials or anaesthetic masks or equipment. Nor was there a trained nurse, but among the passengers was a 17-year-old girl who was travelling to England for nursing training. She offered to help.

Bed sheets were cut up to use as surgical swabs and dressings and I made an anaesthetic mask with wire covered by a small sheet of cotton. The only general anaesthetic substances were bottles of ether and a bottle of ethyl chloride. Ether was one of the first general anaesthetics ever developed but amongst the safest and most easily administered agents. My main concern, however, was about how slow it was likely to be in anaesthetising a fit young man who might resist someone holding a mask over his face. Ethyl-chloride is a much quicker but more potent anaesthetic agent but with little latitude between what amount is safe and effective and what is too much and therefore dangerous. I checked with my volunteer anaesthetist that he knew how to use each agent effectively and safely. I explained that only a little ethyl-chloride should be dropped onto the anaesthetic mask to settle the patient reasonably quickly then this should be followed by a steady, more continuous drip of ether to maintain unconsciousness. He assured me he was familiar with all this so the captain pointed the ship in the best direction for smooth sailing and preparations for the operations began. I had arranged for my very sensible bedroom steward to be my surgical assistant and the young girl to be 'scrub-nurse' helper.

I helped them scrub and put on surgical gloves and explained the importance of totally sterile techniques, emphasising that they must not touch anything that wasn't sterile. Then I put my first patient to sleep with the ethyl-chloride/ether anaesthetic. When the patient was satisfactorily anaesthetised I handed over the anaesthetic duties to the elderly doctor while I scrubbed, gloved, and began the surgery. After I'd made the surgical incision it became apparent that the doctor giving the anaesthetic was having some trouble. In fact our patient was blue and had stopped breathing so I took off my gloves and resuscitated him. I explained to the doctor that I thought he had given too much ethyl chloride and that he should not give any more, just keep slowly dripping ether onto the mask; just enough to keep the patient asleep but not enough to depress his breathing. I then rescrubbed and continued with the operation.

Sure enough the appendix was very acutely inflamed but before I removed it I noticed that the patient had stopped breathing.

Once again I stopped operating and resuscitated the patient. I then insisted that the patient must not be given any more ethyl chloride but the anaesthetising doctor was very unhappy. He said that in his experience he had found ethyl chloride to be a safe anaesthetic agent but that ether should be used sparingly because it was dangerous. I demanded that the ethyl chloride be taken from the operating room and finished the operation without further incident.

Because the other young man still needed an emergency appendectomy we prepared our 'theatre' again, this time banning the elderly doctor from the operating room. I promoted my bedroom steward from assistant to anaesthetist and showed him how to give a safe anaesthetic; the young nurse-to-be filled the vacancy as operating assistant and another young steward became the theatre 'scrub-nurse'. This time the operation went very smoothly with each participant performing his/her role admirably. An equally acutely inflamed appendix was safely removed and we all breathed a sigh of relief.

What I had not catered for was the reception that we all received when we left the operating room with the news that all was well. The word must have passed around the ship that all this was going on and a big celebration that involved passengers and crew broke out. The captain presided over the festivities and after that I could do no wrong. I was invited to more celebratory parties than I could accept and accepted more invitations than were good for me.

One side issue of all this was that one of our passengers was Señor Juan Quadros who was president-elect of Brazil and was travelling with his wife and two lovely daughters (aged 20 and 17) to political events in Europe. Señor Quadros asked me if I would be interested in a medical position in Brazil as his surgeon and surgeon to the Diplomatic Corps in Brazil. He assured me that if I accepted such a position I would make enough money in just five years to retire comfortably for the rest of my life. I was flattered by the suggestion but there were three very good reasons why I gave it no serious thought: first I was in love with Lillian; second I believed it was time I settled down to serious surgical studies and training; and third, I realised that it all depended on Señor Quadros being appointed president and holding the presidency for five years. South American presidents were often removed, one-way or another after short periods in office. (It so happened that Señor Quadros was no exception. He did become president of Brazil, and I understand he was a very good president, but his reform program was blocked by people in powerful positions with vested interests and he resigned in frustration after only seven months in office.)

Ballads at sea

On board my last voyage was a well-spoken, well-educated, classy, and very pregnant woman who expressed gratitude to me for caring for her throughout the journey. As a parting gift she gave me a record that she described as 'a record of ballads' that I took to my friends John and Lois Willis's home in London. John and Lois were old friends from my church youth fellowship in Sydney. Much to my astonishment the 'ballads' were a number of the dirtiest ditties I had ever heard. I choked with embarrassment after each song and hoped that I had just imagined a double meaning to the words but they got worse and worse. Fortunately my friends, although surprised, were not really bothered. They have since reminded me of the event and have asked if I have any more seagoing classics.

A tempting offer

On arrival back in England in the autumn of 1957 I had to make an important decision. Not only was I invited to continue as surgeon in the Royal Mail Line but I was invited to the Cunard Line and asked if I would like a job as surgeon on the *Queen Elizabeth* or *Queen Mary*, giant passenger liners that had regular routes between London and New York and carried large numbers of first-class, second-class and tourist-class passengers. As senior surgeon on either liner I would be primarily responsible for the wealthy first-class passengers and would have the right to charge them private fees.

The prospect was tempting but I realised my choice was whether to become a professional sea-faring wealthy medical playboy (with a distinct risk of becoming an alcoholic) or to seriously continue training to be a qualified surgeon. I am sure I made the right decision in declining the appointment. With a starry-eyed ambition I opted to make the choice I knew was more important, the one I thought would bring me more fulfilment: to get the best training I could in preparation for caring for sick people in my home country. I also knew it was the choice that would have given most satisfaction to my mum and dad.

Scotland

I accepted a position for which I had applied as surgical registrar at the Aberdeen Royal Infirmary, the major teaching hospital of Britain's oldest medical school and I packed up my trusty old SS Jaguar and headed north for Scotland. Because the position wouldn't become vacant for three months I accepted a three-month temporary position as surgical registrar in a hospital in Arbroath, a town that lies on the East Coast of Scotland between Edinburgh and Aberdeen. Arbroath was a good place to work and the appointment allowed me to settle back into the discipline of being a member of a good surgical team. After three pleasant months in Arbroath I moved to Aberdeen.

In my first week in Aberdeen the temperature fell to 27 degrees below freezing point. My faithful old car slipped and slid on the icy, snow-covered roads and I had to use one hand to scratch a small patch on the windscreen to see through because every breath I exhaled immediately froze on the glass. The contrast with so recently having travelled through the tropics was so stark that I was tempted to resign. But I decided to stay, at least for a while, and gradually became acclimatised.

I soon learnt that the best place to be in the north of Scotland at that time of the year was the heated atmosphere of my hospital or in the warm hospitality of my lodgings. I found a place to stay with some other young hospital doctors in the private home of a delightful-middle aged Scottish lady, Miss Hay, who had been recommended as providing comfortable accommodation for hospital doctors living away from home. It was a little like the friendship of my digs when I was at Sydney Boys High School except that there was no shortage of food and Miss Hay was very kind. I was also lucky in that she had a special motherly fondness for Australians. One thing I learnt later was that she would not accept any women boarders and did not approve of 'her boys' becoming involved with members of the opposite sex. She described all young women as 'flippant little hussies'.

Language and pronunciation difficulties

My position in the Royal Infirmary was a 'rotating surgical traineeship', a role that was organised so that I spent three months in each of several specialist surgical units; orthopaedic surgery, neurosurgery, paediatric surgery, head and neck surgery/radiotherapy, and general abdominal surgery. My first three-month term was in orthopaedics. On the first day, in the outpatient orthopaedic clinic, I asked my first patient to tell me about her trouble. The answer I got was, 'Och Doctor it's the stoonin in the hinches'. I tried again but got the same answer so I called in an interpreter who explained that, 'stoonin in the hinches' was highland dialect for 'aching in the hips'. I then realised that to work in the Highland Region of Scotland I needed to learn a new language.

I later discovered that language and pronunciation could present 'two-way' difficulties. It was my practice to dictate my clinical letters to doctors onto a tape recorder for the unit secretaries to type. On one occasion I believed I had said, 'I thought this man's abdominal pain may have been related to his constipation'. When I was given the letter to sign it read, 'I thought this man's abdominal pain might have been related to his constant passion'. On another occasion, I believed I had said, 'this lady had a suspicious skin lesion on her breast so I thought that I should nip it in the bud'. But when the letter was given to me to sign, it read, 'this lady had a suspicious skin lesion on her breast so I thought I should nip it in the bed'.

My term in head and neck surgery with radiotherapy was unique. My chief was Mr Jimmy Phillip (in Britain, and sometimes in Australia, surgeons use the title mister rather than doctor). Mr Phillip was a qualified radiotherapist as well as a highly skilled head and neck surgeon. I learnt from him both the skills of operating on head and neck cancers and the place of radiotherapy in treating head and neck cancers. More than that I learnt the place and value of integrating operative treatment with radiotherapy to achieve better treatment outcomes. This term with Mr Phillip was most rewarding and made an impression with me that remained for the rest of my clinical life.

A chance encounter with British aristocracy

During my paediatric term I received a telephone call from a sporting-field to advise that Lord 'So and So' was being brought in with a broken arm. I wondered why he was being brought in to the children's hospital but he turned out to be a seven year-old boy. I think he was a Marquis of somewhere or other, but he was a nice little fellow with very pleasant parents who waited their turn for me to attend their son. With a greenstick fracture he needed only a plaster cast.

Surgical rotations

I enjoyed each of my surgical rotations and could have specialised in any one of them including paediatric surgery. Being able to help children appealed to me until I had some sad experiences with two or three lovely little kiddies with leukaemia who in those days had no hope of recovery. The experience was so heart-wrenching that I abandoned any thought of a career in Paediatric Surgery.

Other experiences in and out of Scotland

In Aberdeen I was invited to the British Medical Association's Hospital Doctors' Forum. A volunteer was needed to represent the North-East of Scotland at a conference in London. No-one else wanted to go, so I was asked. I could see nothing wrong with an all-expenses-paid round trip to London although I said that I would be suspected of being an impostor as a representative of north-east of Scotland as soon as I opened my mouth. However, I agreed to go and when I began to speak there were some comments made and general amusement, but I was warmly welcomed and a good time was had by all.

When I left Aberdeen I parked my car in a big railway yard (which seemed the best place) and caught the train to London. A few days later when I returned by train I found a very tired-looking policeman standing by my car to serve me a parking penalty for illegal parking. Apparently parking fines in Scotland had to be served personally. I was fined two pounds but thought that I had had good value for my money having apparently procured police protection for my car for several days at a cost of only two pounds.

In 1958, after rotating through the special surgical units in Orthopaedic Surgery, Neurosurgery, Gastro-intestinal Surgery, Paediatric Surgery, Head and Neck Cancer Surgery with

Radiotherapy, all of which I enjoyed and learned from, I was appointed surgical registrar in 'the Professorial unit' that was headed by Professor Wilson (shortly to retire) and two young senior lecturers, Hugh Dudley and James Kyle. In those days Professors were like God. Professor Wilson was a nice man but I never heard him called by his first name and I still don't know what it was. Everyone stood to attention when he walked into a room and everyone, even the other surgeons, always addressed him as 'sir'. It was under the supervision of the two brilliant young surgeons, Hugh Dudley and James Kyle, both of whom were originally from Northern Ireland, that I completed most of my practical as well as theoretical surgical training. They were both surgical dynamos with a special interest in abdominal surgery but were both able to cope with any difficult surgical problem. The offer to be registrar in the Professorial unit was just what I wanted, although I have since regretted that I had not had experience in either the vascular surgical unit or the thoracic surgical unit. These have always since been surgical areas where I thought it best to refer any difficult problems to a more experienced thoracic surgeon or vascular surgeon.

Research – Outpatient Surgery, 1958–1960

When I was first appointed registrar to the Professor of Surgery I was told I would be required not only to give some lectures to students and nurses but I was expected to carry out a research program as well. I was to help the senior lecturers, Dudley and Kyle, in their research into the causes, physiology and treatment of gastric and duodenal ulcers – but the Professor also asked me whether I had any particular research in mind as my own special project.

I had been getting a fair experience in abdominal surgery but I wanted to get as much operative surgery experience as possible. As the Royal Infirmary was a regional hospital covering most of the north-east of Scotland at that time, the non-urgent 'elective' surgical waiting lists were very long, especially for varicose-vein or hernia operations, where delays of three years were standard. I had been impressed to learn that a well-known surgeon in Edinburgh was being successful in reducing the Edinburgh Royal Infirmary waiting list by operating on some suitable patients with hernias or varicose veins under local anaesthesia and allowing many of them to go home the same day. This was a significant advance in reducing his surgical waiting list that had resulted from a shortage of hospital beds. He carefully selected his patients for this procedure, because not all patients were suitable or willing to have their operations under local anaesthesia. I was also well aware that in many other countries including America and Australia and several European countries, children who had tonsillectomies under general anaesthesia were often allowed to go home on the same day as their operations. Finally, I was encouraged by the proposal of some American clinics that some patients having surgery under a general anaesthetic would be discharged into an adjacent hostel accommodation within a day or two of their surgery. All this accumulating evidence led me to believe that with special care it should be possible to perform surgical operations on adults under general anaesthesia on an 'outpatient' or 'day stay' basis which, if successful, would reduce patients' waiting times for hospital beds for non-urgent operations, as well as greatly reduce government health costs. The immediate bonuses for me were that I would have a lot more operating experience and be involved in much needed research of potential great value to health budgets the world over. I also believed that there might be less wound infection in operation wounds in patients who had not mixed with hospital 'inpatients', some of whom might have infected wounds or other infections.

The Professor subsequently agreed to my proposal to conduct a study into the practicality of 'Outpatient' or 'Day-stay' surgery and the idea was strongly supported by both senior lecturers. Hugh Dudley agreed to help as much as possible by supervising the study and arranging the cooperation of anaesthetists and other members of staff as well as patients' family doctors and the ambulance teams needed to take them home after they had recovered from their anaesthetics. With the help and co-operation of many people, especially two anaesthetist colleagues, the project was highly successful. A full report was written by Hugh Dudley and myself and was published in *The Lancet* on 15 May 1961. In that publication we predicted: 'Adoption of schemes of this kind might do much to relieve the unrelenting pressure on surgical beds'. I am proud that this was the forerunner of many similar studies in many parts of the world and 'Outpatient' or 'Day Stay' surgery under general anaesthetic has become established worldwide to the benefit of patients as well as government budgets and health systems. My only disappointment is that our work planned, performed and published by an Australian surgical registrar with the help of a Northern Irish surgical lecturer in a Scottish hospital has rarely been recognised anywhere as the forerunner of this now common cost-saving surgical practice that also has the benefit of less risk of wound infection.

After a term in the Professorial unit I was made an unusual offer that saw me elevated to the position of senior surgical registrar in the Professorial unit. I was approached by an extremely wealthy American (one of the Woolworth family) who had converted a very seaworthy Scottish fishing trawler into a small but luxurious passenger ship. However he had a health problem and wanted a surgeon to travel with him on his first trip across the Atlantic to America. He had heard of my shipboard experience and I was invited to accept this position, but completion of my surgical training and research in the Aberdeen University Professorial Surgical Unit was my priority. I discussed the offer with the Professorial senior surgical registrar, Mr Ainslie Anderson. Ainslie had completed his surgical training and wanted to go to America to take up a research position. He proposed that if I turned down the passage and recommended him for the job, he would happily recommend me for the resulting vacancy as senior registrar to the Professor that would result from his resignation. It seemed like a good deal all around and we put the wheels in motion. However, before my appointment as senior surgical registrar could go ahead it was important for me to pass the final surgical fellowship examination for the Royal College of Surgeons. I asked the Professor for leave to go to London to complete the final fellowship examination. He rebuked me saying, 'No laddie, you will not be going south of Edinburgh. You must become a fellow of the Royal College of Surgeons of Edinburgh,' clearly revealing the on-going rivalry between the different Royal Colleges. I passed my final examination in Edinburgh, much to the satisfaction of the Professor and incidentally saved myself the effort and expense of going to London.

Lillian and Alison

During this period I received some letters from Lillian in New York and although I replied to her regularly, she kept asking about my work and life in Scotland as if she had not received them. I only had the one address for her there and I didn't have a telephone number and so eventually her letters became less frequent and began to include questions and complaints about my not having written. In the meantime I became involved in a quite lively social life.

One evening I went to a university dance at Aberdeen's renowned university college, the Marshall College. It was there that I noticed a real beauty with a group of my friends and somehow I managed to make contact with her and we exchanged telephone numbers. Soon we were dating regularly and enjoying a passionate love life. Her name was Alison and she came from Dufftown in the highlands: a major settlement in the malt whisky region of Scotland.

Alison's beauty was enhanced by her freckles which I loved; to me she became 'Freckle Face'. Soon 'Freckle Face' invited me home to meet her parents and over the next few months I spent several weekends as a guest of her family. Within two miles of the centre of Dufftown there are nine malt whisky distilleries which produce such famous brands of Scotch as Glenfiddich (Scotland's largest malt whisky distillery), Glen Grant, Glenlivet and Mortlach.

Whenever we attended church with Alison's parents we would often be invited to someone's home for 'tea or coffee'. I soon learnt that the 'tea or coffee' usually came out of an unlabelled bottle the contents of which were indistinguishable from malt whisky and although the output of all distilleries was subject to customs duty, an allowance of six per cent was made for evaporation and spillage. However, the real rate of evaporation and spillage was around three per cent and so the remainder was distributed around the town in unlabelled bottles.

In Dufftown I learnt to appreciate the qualities of good malt whisky and especially that adding anything to it, such as soda or water or ice, only contaminated it. Although I am only a very moderate drinker I still enjoy a good malt whisky as long as it has not been thus contaminated. Since then only seven of my close friends have ever shared my appreciation of a good, pure, uncontaminated Scotch malt whisky. One of these was Alan Somerville, a grateful former patient who made sure that my malt whisky supply was reinforced every birthday and every Christmas. Two other aficionados are my sisters-in-law Frances and Patricia Kelly, and the most recent is my son-in-law Rob Williams. Sadly my personal 'malt whisky fan club' was depleted by the death of my American surgical mentor and friend Dr Bert Dunphy, and more recently by the death of Malcolm Inglis, a distinguished Sydney Hospital surgical colleague and friend. It was Malcolm who introduced me to a very special lowland Scotch malt whisky called Glenkinchie – a whisky of special flavour indeed. The last of the 'malt-taster' seven is an eminent Professor of Surgery in Israel, Professor Gur Ben-Ari but distance makes it a long time between drinks with him unless we happen to be speaking on the same conference program somewhere in the world.

In the autumn of 1959 I suddenly and unexpectedly was allowed a couple of weeks' holiday. Alison and I had been talking about getting married and we decided that while there was time we should have a honeymoon. We decided to have a camping holiday around the highlands of Scotland, including especially the West Coast and the Isle of Skye. A few weeks later Alison was surprised to discover that she was pregnant, and that our baby was due the following July. There was no time for a Dufftown wedding so I confided in my surgical boss Hugh Dudley and his wife Jean. Hugh arranged for me to have a few days off over Christmas and Alison and I were married on Christmas Eve 1959 in a lovely little church by a stream in the centre of Scotland in the beautiful village of Pitlochry. We spent the night in Pitlochry and drove next day to Dufftown where we surprised Alison's parents on Christmas Day with news of our wedding. I was delighted that they reacted with great joy. They called friends and neighbours over to celebrate and share their pleasure with us.

However, it was not all plain sailing. Before my marriage to Alison was even a week old I had a telephone call from Lillian who had come to London to track me down because she had not received any of my letters. I was overcome with emotion and had to explain to her that I had just got married and I could not therefore come to London to be with her. We realised that the reason none of my letters had arrived was that we wrote the number '7' differently. Her habit was to cross the vertical line. The number 4 that I had been writing in several places in her address was really meant to be number 7. In South America the number 7 is usually crossed to look like a 4 but in Australia it is not. I had been mailing her letters to the wrong address for two years. Sad though this was for all of us, especially for Lillian, I could not undo the fact that I had a pregnant wife expecting our first baby in seven months time.

Our beautiful baby daughter, Jennifer, was born in Aberdeen on 30 June 1960, and christened in an old family church in Dufftown with Hugh and Jean Dudley as godparents. Towards the end of my year as Senior Registrar in Aberdeen I had decided that further research would be my priority before settling into practice.

Portland, Oregon: Dr J. Englebert Dunphy

The best place to obtain research experience was America. Hugh Dudley told me he had worked in Boston with a brilliant American surgeon, Dr J. Englebert Dunphy, a Professor at Harvard University. Since working with Hugh, Dr Dunphy had moved to Portland, Oregon, as Professor and Head of the Department of Surgery in the Oregon University School of Medicine, a relatively small but excellent medical school. I contacted Dr Dunphy who advised me that there was a competitive research fellowship, the 'Joyce Fellowship', for which I could apply. He also suggested that I should also apply for a 'Wellcome' travelling fellowship to pay for travel expenses for my wife and baby as well as myself.

I was fortunate to be awarded both of these fellowships so Alison and I and baby Jenny set off across the Atlantic. We sailed on the *Queen Elizabeth*, the same ocean liner I had declined to join as ship's surgeon nearly four years previously to take up the position in Aberdeen. We enjoyed the journey and had an interesting couple of days in New York at the height of the Kennedy/Nixon election campaign. While sightseeing we came across several open-air election rallies with all the attendant hoopla that is an inevitable part of American election campaigns. At times we felt like we were the only people in New York not wearing a donkey, an elephant or a Nixon or Kennedy badge, and we continually found ourselves being encouraged to join rallies or to vote one way or the other.

On our arrival in Portland we were met by one of Dr Dunphy's senior medical students, Dick Scott, who had arranged comfortable accommodation for us in a unit quite close to the medical school.

Alison and I became good friends with Dick and his wife Linda over the next few months. Dick introduced us to Gilbert and Sullivan operettas through his involvement with an amateur theatre company, and Gilbert and Sullivan theatre became a favourite of mine.

Dr Dunphy invited me to work on any research project that interested me. I therefore organised studies on bile-duct surgery, a special interest of Dr Dunphy, and set up a project on cancer treatment that was of particular interest to me.

It was my first introduction to cancer research. I discovered that something in the white of hens' eggs slowed the rate of growth of various cancers implanted into mice. However, as much as I tried I could not find any particular ingredient that was responsible for this pronounced reduction of cancer-cell growth, but I now suspect that it might have stimulated an immune response. (This study was published in 1964 in the prestigious medical journal, *The Lancet*.)

Our papers on bile duct repair were also published in American surgical journals. Both of these studies led to Dr Dunphy and me being invited to present our work at several American surgical meetings.

Nearing the end of our time in Portland I heard about a vacancy for a senior lectureship position in the Department of Surgery at Sydney University. Dr Dunphy had invited me to accept a very good position in Portland, but much as it appealed to me I really wanted to return to Australia to join my old medical school and especially to bring up our children. I applied for and was appointed to the Sydney University senior lectureship in surgery with a clinical appointment at Sydney's Royal Prince Alfred Hospital. While celebrating my new appointment I asked Dr Dunphy if he would consider bringing Mrs Dunphy to Sydney and be my first guest Professor if I were ever in a position to invite him. He happily promised to accept any such invitation.

Our year in Portland had been a happy one. Dr Dunphy was an excellent surgeon, researcher, teacher and boss and we became good friends. But the happiest event of our year there was the birth of our first boy, Robert Bruce Henry Stephens (4.7 kg). Alison and I now had an international family, two Scots (Alison and Jenny), one Australian (me) and one American (Bobby).

Chapter Three

Return to Sydney

In December 1961, after eight years and a rich and varied international medical and surgical experience I returned to my hometown with my new family. In Sydney Mum and Dad and my brothers and sisters and some friends met us. My brother Bruce had arranged a rented house for us in Abbotsford that was handy to the hospital and the university. It was a very happy homecoming.

Two memorable meetings

After returning to Sydney I met two very interesting – and very different – doctors. One was World War II hero 'Weary' Dunlop (later Sir Edward) and the other was Christian Barnard, who was visiting Sydney in 1967 shortly after he had performed the world's first heart transplant in his native South Africa.

Weary Dunlop VC

Weary dined with Alison and me after I had a phone call from my boss John Loewenthal informing us that Dr Dunlop had missed his plane departing Sydney and asking us to entertain him for a few hours. We picked him up and took him to our modest home for dinner. It was a most happy and memorable experience.

After distinguishing himself in caring for his fellow prisoners in a horrific Japanese war camp, Dr Dunlop had returned from the war and gone on to become a highly regarded surgeon practising in Melbourne. I had known that he had been a prominent Australian Rules football player, but I had not known that he was also a very skilled, all-round sportsman. Although reluctant to talk about himself, I gradually teased some sporting information from him. For fun he had tried out for rugby and apparently after just 16 games he was selected in an Australian Rugby Union representative team. I often saw Weary at surgical meetings in his latter years. Then honoured with a knighthood, Sir Edward Dunlop always sought me out for a chat. He always asked how my work was progressing, always encouraging me to continue. At one meeting I had my doctor son Bobby with me. Bobby was delighted to meet this great man, Weary remained a most humble and gracious man until he died in 1993.

Christian Barnard

When famous heart transplant surgeon Christian Barnard visited Sydney Professor Loewenthal was away so I was detailed to be his host for a week or so. I was to arrange his speaking engagements, introduce him to his audiences, and arrange to take him to a celebration ball. Ignorant of his reputation as a ladies man, I asked him to the ball, an offer he enthusiastically accepted. It soon became apparent both on and off the dance floor that Dr Barnard was effusive in his attentions and advances to the opposite sex, including my wife Alison. He had been an interesting visitor but I was glad to wave him goodbye next morning.

When I began work with Professor John Loewenthal at the Royal Prince Alfred Hospital in Sydney my two special interests were in cancer surgery and gastroenterology. But since Sydney was well provided with surgeons interested in gastroenterology, and being mindful of Dr Shuttleworth's words at St Thomas's Hospital in London several years previously that 'cancer is our greatest unsolved health problem', I concentrated on cancer surgery. It worked well because my boss, Professor John Loewenthal, specialised in vascular surgery, a field in which his registrars were all well trained, while I worked closely with the hospital's other specialist in cancer treatment, the radiotherapist Dr David Green. In those days cancer was always treated either by a surgeon or a radiotherapist but studies were beginning to identify medical treatments that were effective in treating some cancers. Although doctors had been trying to find drugs to cure cancer for centuries, the first effective anticancer drug, nitrogen mustard, was discovered only serendipitously when a gas used in war was studied as a potential weapon in World

War II. In animal experiments it had been observed that when the agent was injected into the bloodstream the white blood cells were depressed. This drug was then trialled in some patients with leukaemia. Although it had a good temporary response in many cases, there was a risk of serious side-effects. When it was later trialled in some patients with other cancers there were some encouraging responses, but there was always a risk of serious side-effects, especially depression of white blood cells.

These were the early days of cancer chemotherapy. By the time I arrived back in Sydney, haematologists were using new anti-cancer drugs with some success against leukaemias and some widespread cancers, but when surgeons or radiotherapists used the same drugs the results were disappointing. What surgeons and radiotherapists most needed were drugs that could effectively treat cancers that had recurred after previous surgery or radiotherapy had failed to cure the cancer.

Some years earlier, two American medical journals had reported the same accidental discovery by two surgeons working independently: when someone had intended to inject a new anti-cancer agent into a vein in front of the elbow joint, the drug had accidentally been injected into an artery and this had provoked a considerable reaction in the hand and tissues that the artery was supplying. Both surgeons postulated that the anti-cancer drug might be more effective if, rather than being injected into a vein, it was injected into an artery that directly supplied a cancer with blood. This made sense to me since any agent injected into a vein would be diluted by its passage around the body before reaching the target cancer. I wondered if this could be a clue to more effective treatment of some cancers?

Several surgeons in different parts of the world had similar thoughts. They believed that chemotherapy might be more effective if it was delivered more directly to a cancer by injecting it into the artery supplying blood to the cancer. I persuaded Professor Loewenthal to investigate the effect of injecting anti-cancer drugs into arteries that supplied blood to cancers that were considered too big to be cured by surgery or by radiotherapy. I hoped the treatment would shrink the cancers so that surgery or radiotherapy could then be used to 'finish it off'.

Unfortunately results were disappointing both in our department and in other departments that tried the same approach. So Professor Loewenthal, like most surgeons, lost interest in further researching this area, and in using any of the new anti-cancer drugs. However, I was convinced the principle was right and that there must have been something that we had overlooked. I was determined to continue studies in this area if and when I had my own unit.

In November 1962 our third child, Jill (Gillian Dorys Janet), was born. She was the first Australian-born, and the first of our children to inherit the prominent Stephens family red-headedness gene. We felt very blessed.

A political minefield

In 1962 the University of Sydney had been having some political and administrative troubles with Sydney Hospital, its oldest teaching hospital. The hospital directors believed that the university had neglected Sydney Hospital for some years. They threatened to leave Sydney University and join the newly established University of New South Wales unless Sydney University took a greater interest by allocating funds for the hospital to be modernised and upgraded. In a gesture of appeasement, Professor Loewenthal arranged for me to be the founding representative of a Sydney University unit in surgery at Sydney Hospital. So, at 34 years of age I was appointed Associate Professor in Surgery to establish an academic surgical unit in Sydney hospital. The Professor suggested that as I had been a student at Sydney Hospital I would have the best chance of 'appeasing the difficult Sydney Hospital monsters', but he didn't like my chances because they were an 'impossible lot' who didn't know what they wanted. He said I could always come back to the Royal Prince Alfred Hospital if, as he expected, my new challenge failed.

Early in 1963 therefore, with some fear and trepidation, I took up my new appointment as Associate Professor of Surgery at my old teaching hospital. My darling mother would have been so proud but sadly she had died quite suddenly just a few weeks before my appointment and only three weeks before our daughter Gillian was born. She died of an acute episode of long-standing cardiac asthma. I was glad that I had returned to Australia in time for her to meet my wife and two children before she died, but I was also sorry that she had not lived to see me appointed Associate Professor at Sydney Hospital. Like me, she believed that Sydney Hospital was the best in the country.

Sydney Hospital

In spite of the misgivings expressed by Professor Loewenthal, and after a little initial suspicion of the political purpose behind my appointment, I was warmly welcomed at the hospital. My colleagues were especially proud when a few years later I was elected president of the Surgical Research Society of Australasia in recognition of research studies I established there. Most of the junior and some of the senior staff with whom I published research papers had never previously taken part in a research study or had a paper published.

Sydney Hospital was under constant threat from governments because it occupied the best piece of real estate in Sydney. It was adjacent to the state parliament house, and successive state governments had plans to expand onto the hospital grounds. The uncertainty over its future resulted in a lack of substantial infrastructure funding, and the hospital was therefore allowed to physically deteriorate in the hope that its directors would agree to it being rebuilt somewhere else.

In fact the deterioration of the buildings and facilities may have contributed to the highly developed loyalties of Sydney Hospital's staff: everyone supported each other in making best use of the poor physical facilities while still maintaining the highest standards of medical care. Sydney Hospital had, and still has, the most cordial group of staff members with whom I have ever worked. I remain close friends with many of the people I first met there.

Moving to Mosman

As Associate Professor at Sydney Hospital, it was important for me to live where I could be readily available for emergencies. We found a house within our price range in Mosman on Sydney's North shore. It was quite modest but it had many advantages. It was reasonably close to Sydney Hospital, and it was in a good area for children, with schools, parks and a beach nearby. (Quite incidentally I discovered some years later that my mother's mother, Sarah Mosman, was a member of the Mosman family to which a large area of land was granted and in which the suburb of Mosman was established).

Not long after we moved into our new home in Mosman Alison became pregnant with our son Peter. At the same time my brother Stan's wife, Shirley, who lived in a country town, was having troubles in the late stages of her pregnancy and moved in with us to be close to specialist obstetrical services. Neighbours have since told me they had wondered what was going on when this new bloke moved in with a bunch of kids and two heavily pregnant women both calling themselves Mrs Stephens.

As a child I had always had a dog and Alison and I agreed that we should have one both as a pet and protector for our children. After a lot of deliberation we decided on a labrador, a breed that is very good with children but which is also a good watchdog. We decided to buy a female pedigreed bitch that would provide our children with valuable – and free – sex education and also be suitable for breeding should we ever want puppies. The kids loved their dog, but this addition to the family was soon overshadowed by the birth of our fourth child, Frederick William Peter, in September 1964.

Dr Dunphy – Guest Professor

Every year the Sydney Hospitallers held a reunion for a week at which we had a program of research and clinical papers as well as social functions. A different 'visiting Professor' was invited each year and in 1965 I was asked to nominate a visiting Professor. Our visiting Professors were expected to give some lectures and to attend the hospital for five or six weeks to teach students and junior staff, so it was with some trepidation that I invited Dr Dunphy. I knew it wouldn't be easy for him to accept the invitation because he had just been invited to become head of the Department of Surgery at the University of California in San Francisco, a much bigger department than he had in Portland. Nevertheless, as he had promised four years earlier, he accepted my invitation. He and his wife, Nancy, became our guests and lived in the hospitality flat at Sydney Hospital for five weeks while he met his commitments as guest Professor.

The Flying Doctor

Dr Dunphy asked me to show him something of 'the Outback' and the Royal Flying Doctor Service, so on the 1965 Easter weekend we flew to Broken Hill where I had arranged to meet with the then 'Flying Doctor', Graham Ambrose.

On our first night we were having dinner with Dr Ambrose when his emergency phone rang. A man had wrapped his car around a tree at high speed in the little town of Wilcannia, more than a hundred miles north-east of Broken Hill. It was too dark for the doctor's plane to take off so arrangements were made for a flight as soon as there was sufficient daylight. We were keen to accompany Dr Ambrose, who explained that the little plane could carry only four people so Dr Dunphy and I agreed to act as substitute stretcher-bearer and nurse respectively. On the flight I was sitting behind the pilot, Captain Jenkins, when I noticed that one light on the instrument panel was flashing red. Not wanting to appear too apprehensive I asked Captain Jenkins about the function of the many lights and dials. He explained them all except the one that most concerned me. So I asked him directly what that flashing red 'danger' light meant. He answered dryly: 'I'm buggered if I know, I've never seen it do anything else!'.

When we arrived in Wilcannia we were taken to Wilcannia Hospital to find that our patient was severely injured with several fractures. Somehow he had wrapped his car around one of the very few trees in the district and he needed to be transported back to Broken-Hill Base Hospital for surgical attention. When my nursing skill wasn't required I took photos of the great American surgeon acting as a stretcher-bearer. A couple of years later, when I was in San Francisco giving a lecture to Dr Dunphy's surgical trainees I was able to make use of the photographs which I displayed on a screen: 'You young surgeons complain about the qualifications you must have to get a specialist staff job in an American hospital, but look at the qualifications you need to get a job as a stretcher-bearer in outback Australia!' I said. At that time, as well as being their department chief, Dr Dunphy was President of the American College of Surgeons and also President of the International Colleges of Surgeons.

After our visit to Wilcannia Dr Dunphy and I spent the next day with Dr Ambrose attending his radio clinic. It was very impressive. People telephoned in from their remote outback cattle or sheep stations and Dr Ambrose questioned them about their complaints and symptoms and came to a conclusion as to what was the most likely cause of and best treatment for their problems. He would advise them what tablets or medications to take from their medicine chests, and in some cases would arrange to 'drop-by' on his next flight. He also arranged to fly out to pick up one child who may have had acute appendicitis.

The real outback

The chief organiser and host for our visit to Broken Hill was Keith Connors, a sheep and cattle station owner who was a member of the Broken Hill Hospital Board. Keith invited us to spend two more days with him. On the first day he took us to see the vast man-made Menindee Lakes about 160 kilometres east of Broken Hill. The lakes were formed by the overflow from the nearby Darling River into a series of adjoining valleys. They are filled in times of flood and become Broken Hill's water supply and also a major resort and holiday centre for the the city's residents.

On the second day we visited Keith's cattle/sheep station west of Broken Hill. My conversation with Keith went something like this:

'What a pity that your land can't be watered or irrigated'.

'What for?'

'So you could grow more grass.'

'Why would I need more grass?'

'To feed your sheep and cattle.'

'Look at my sheep and cattle, do they look undernourished?'

I looked more closely at the few sheep and cattle I could see moving from one small tuft of grass to another and I had to confess they didn't look undernourished.

'Then why would I want more water?'

'How many sheep do you have?'

'About 16,000.'

'With a bit more grass you could have 30,000 sheep.'

'I couldn't handle 30,000 sheep.'

'How many acres do you have?'

'We don't measure this land in acres. I have about 100 square miles of land.'

'If you had more water you could have all your sheep and cattle on maybe only half that area of land'.

'What would I do with the other half?'

'Sell it to someone else.'

'I wouldn't like that,' he said, 'I like living in the bush, I don't want the place to become bloody overcrowded like the city. My next door neighbour is just down the road, if I need him he is only about 15 miles away. I wouldn't want anyone closer than that.'

Dr Dunphy listened in disbelief; he didn't know whether Keith was serious or not, but I think he was.

After Doctor Dunphy returned to San Francisco I realised that I had learnt more surgery, surgical research and surgical values from him than from anyone else. I am truly indebted to him. A further bonus of his visit was that in Sydney Hospital I introduced him to Bruce Conolly, our Senior Registrar in Surgery. Bruce had an ambition to work in America so I arranged for him to be Dr Dunphy's host during his stay in Sydney Hospital. I also arranged to introduce Dr Dunphy to James May, the Senior Surgical Registrar at the Royal Prince Alfred Hospital. Both Bruce and Jim subsequently spent valuable time in Dr Dunphy's department in San Francisco.

Sydney Hospitallers: Australia Day Dinners

When I began as Associate Professor at Sydney Hospital I was welcomed into the 'Sydney Hospitallers' club which consisted of past and present medical staff and students – and within a few years I was elected its president. This was an honour I cherished and I am proud that as president I made one significant contribution: I began the tradition of holding Sydney Hospital Vice-Regal dinners on Australia Day.

I was initially disappointed to discover that nothing special had ever been done to celebrate the hospital's unique historic role as Australia's first medical institution. Australia Day was of special relevance to Sydney Hospital because it was first established in temporary accommodation near Circular Quay upon the arrival of the First Fleet. It was moved it to its present site in Macquarie Street by Governor Macquarie in 1811. Given this I suggested to my colleagues that we should organise a special dinner on Australia Day, and that we should invite the Governor General as our Guest of Honour.

Through official channels I invited the Governor General Sir

Zelman Cowan to attend. Sir Zelman replied that he would be honoured to accept our invitation. A great dinner was held in the hospital's boardroom with Sir Zelman as guest of honour, and the tradition continued for a number of years thereafter, with a series of Governors General, State Governors and other appropriate distinguished celebrities as guests of honour.

The dinners became a highlight in the Sydney Hospital calendar, but regretfully the tradition died some years later after interference from the New South Wales Minister for Health, Laurie Brereton; the hospital's most highly specialised units and staff were transferred to another location.

In those days I was not aware of the personal dislike and professional rivalry between my boss, Professor John Loewenthal and the Sydney Hospital president Dr Frank Ritchie. Consequently John Loewenthal was never invited to the Australia Day dinners, over which Frank Ritchie always presided. I think this may have increased the distrust between the teaching hospital and its parent university and I, as initiator of the Vice-Regal dinners, was apparently seen as a party to Professor Loewenthal's exclusion. Because Professor Loewenthal demanded loyalty he thereafter regarded me as disloyal to him and therefore to the university. He regarded his opinions and image and the university opinions and image as one and the same thing.

Dr Bill Larkins

While I received support in my work from several medical organizations and practising specialists, including senior members of the British Medical Association (later to become the Australian Medical Association), none was as important as the British Medical Association's NSW secretary Dr Nicholas (Bill) Larkins. Bill visited the hospital to see and take an interest in my work and encouraged others to do so as well. He read my published papers and inspired me to write and research more and to nurture additional research in others. Bill, Sir Keith Jones, the National President of the BMA, and Dr Ted Booth the NSW branch President, also invited me to accept a vacancy on the Council of the NSW branch of the AMA and to join its surgical and research working committees.

Bill also introduced me to the treasurer of the AMA's NSW

branch, Dr John Bain, the first family doctor to live and establish a practice in the Kurmond/Kurrajong district. John was a returned serviceman, having served with distinction in the jungles of New Guinea in World War II. He was a post-war medical graduate who became a popular figure with the district's World War I soldier settlers who were contemporaries of my Dad, as well as the newly returned World War II servicemen and women and their families. John and I remained close friends until his death about three years ago. We had many mutual friends, patients and happy experiences and memories of life in Kurmond and surrounding regions.

A rather flattering appointment that Bill Larkins and others asked me to accept was to be on stand-by every time an important royal or political figure visited Sydney. This was a considerable honour which I happily accepted. I was subsequently surgeon on duty for the visit of HRH the Duke of Edinburgh in 1965; the President of the United States, President Lyndon Johnson in 1966; Her Majesty the Queen and HRH the Duke of Edinburgh during their visit in 1967 and I was also appointed surgeon on duty for the visits of Prince Charles, the Shah of Persia (now Iran), the Crown Prince of Japan and the King and Queen of Nepal during their visits to Sydney.

Opening the Sydney Opera House

In 1973 the Queen visited Sydney to open the Sydney Opera House. I was appointed her personal surgeon during this visit and was required to be in ready attendance at the opening of the Opera House. Alison and I were allocated two seats in full view of the Royal Party during the opening-night concert. It was an occasion that I will never forget.

During each visit from overseas dignitaries my children hoped that one of the VIPs concerned would have a minor health problem so that my brush with fame might be more meaningful than a polite handshake. To their frustration neither surgical nor medical help was ever required.

Alison and I were sometimes also a little bemused by the media attention that occasionally came our way as a result of my role. I think the social columnists were impressed, not by me, but by my beautiful young Scottish wife, because several times our photographs appeared in the social pages of one or other of the Sunday newspapers. In these photographs it was evident that it was Alison they were interested in. I felt very honoured by these appointments but I did not realise until some time later that they did not please Professor Loewenthal my boss, who thought they should have been given to him.

More political and administrative problems

In 1967 my friend Gerry Milton, the most senior of our Associate Professors at Sydney University Department of Surgery, was due to be promoted to full Professor. For some years John Loewenthal, who was a capable surgeon and a very skilled administrator, had relied on Gerry's strengths in teaching and research. Gerry had been developing a Melanoma Unit at St Vincent's Hospital which Sydney University was in danger of losing with the transfer of St Vincent's Hospital to the newly established University of New South Wales medical school. Sydney Hospital was by then happily re-associated with Sydney University and was the only teaching hospital prepared to accommodate a full chair of surgery so Gerry and his registrar, Bill McCarthy, came to join me in our rather crowded quarters at Sydney Hospital.

Frank Ritchie, the hospital President, and the Sydney Hospital administration were quite resentful of the fact that an Associate Professor from another hospital had been appointed to a Professorial chair in their hospital rather than me, their own Associate Professor whom they had expected to be appointed to the position. However, when they were assured by Professor Loewenthal that the next chair would be for me, Gerry was gradually accepted into the fold. As a result he and Bill further developed their now world-renowned Sydney Melanoma Unit while at Sydney Hospital.

Loewenthal: an administrator extraordinaire

I continued to be impressed by the enthusiasm of my boss for further developing Sydney University clinical schools and his ability to make things happen. Although not everyone was comfortable with Professor Loewenthal's methods, which at times were regarded by some as Machiavellian, he certainly managed to get things done. Perhaps skilled politicking and skilled administration are the same thing. I was aware of Professor Loewenthal's ambition to become

Dean of the university's Faculty of Medicine, so without his knowledge I spoke to a number of people including the retiring Dean, and to Professor Gerry Milton, to secure their support for his nomination for the Deanship. Following his appointment as Dean he continued to excel in building the faculty's reputation and further developing the sub-units in all the university's major teaching hospitals.

Later Gerry Milton and I thought it would be appropriate for Professor Loewenthal to be honoured for his hard work and administrative skills and we secretly nominated him for a knighthood, then Australia's highest accolade. Our nomination was successful. His new title seemed to bestow upon him even greater authority in making administrative decisions.

It was a disappointment that my efforts to have Bill Larkins awarded a knighthood for his wonderful contributions to medicine were not successful. My nomination of Dr Larkins for this honour was supported by no less than Cardinal James Freeman who had been an old school friend of Bill Larkins. Cardinal Freeman very graciously welcomed me to visit him to discuss this project. He enthusiastically supported it. I don't know if the authorities approached Bill but it is sad that his extraordinary contributions to medicine were not appropriately acknowledged in his lifetime.

A breakthrough in treatment sequences for difficult cancers

When I joined Sydney Hospital no-one specialised exclusively in cancer surgery, and the hospital's well-respected surgeon, Dr Stan Spencer, whose special interest was in surgery of the head and neck, had recently retired. Because several of the established surgeons were interested in gastrointestinal surgery which had been the main area of my training team in Aberdeen I decided to concentrate on re-establishing a service in head-and-neck surgery and cancer surgery.

In doing this I was pleased to have an opportunity to apply some of the skills I had learnt from Mr Phillip in Aberdeen several years previously. As a major part of head and neck surgery is cancer surgery I knew that from there I could develop a service in advanced cancer surgery which had not been established in Sydney and which was really my main area of interest.

Effective anti-cancer drugs were being discovered, but in spite of the previous failures in Professor Loewenthal's unit at Royal Prince

Alfred Hospital, I believed there must be an explanation as to why some widespread cancers responded to anti-cancer drugs, while the localised cancers in our surgical patients were not – even when the drugs were concentrated in the cancer region by giving them directly into the artery of supply.

As a surgeon a number of patients were referred to me with advanced cancers in the head-and-neck that had not been cured by radiotherapy or surgery. I tried to make these recurrent cancers smaller, this time using the newer anti-cancer drugs that had been used with increasing success by haematologists. I cooperated closely in these studies with two distinguished doctors on the Sydney Hospital staff, Drs Colin Hambly and Fred Gunz (later appointed Professor Gunz). Colin Hambly was an unusually gifted radiotherapist with a wealth of knowledge and experience in cancer treatment. Fred Gunz was not only an internationally renowned haematologist but he was also director of Sydney Hospital's famous Kanematsu Research Institute, the home of the 1963 Nobel Prize winner in medicine, Sir John Eccles.

Like the studies I had promoted during 1962 in Professor Loewenthal's unit, our early results were disappointing. Even though I infused the drugs directly into the artery supplying the cancer, the cancers were largely unchecked, while side effects were troublesome.

An explanation for the apparently contradictory results of the same new anti-cancer drugs being effective in haematological patients, but ineffective in surgical patients, came to me in 1968 during a visit to my unit by Professor L.B.M. Joseph, Director of the Christian Medical College in Vellore, India. Professor Joseph gave a presentation about his experience treating many previously untreated but very advanced mouth cancers that occur frequently in people who have chewed betel-nut over several years. Like tobacco, betel-nut is a carcinogen. It causes horrible cancers in the mouth that grow through the cheek onto the face. Many of Professor Joseph's patients had arrived from remote Indian villages with very advanced cancers that could not be cured by operation, or radiotherapy, or by a combination of both. Anti-cancer drugs were tried but although they made most cancers smaller there was only a temporary regression. The cancers soon grew even larger than ever.

Professor Joseph and his team then tried using surgery, radiotherapy and chemotherapy, one after the other, in different sequences. They found that using chemotherapy first, radiotherapy second and surgery last, proved more successful than any other sequence. These results made sense to me: chemotherapy is carried directly to the cancer by blood-flow which is damaged by both radiotherapy and surgery. It was logical therefore that chemotherapy was more effective when given before the blood vessels and blood-flow had been damaged by surgery or radiotherapy. Radiotherapy is also more effective in the cancers that have a good blood-flow and therefore it should be most effective if given before a surgeon has interfered with arteries that supply the cancer. This approach also made sense to Drs Hambly and Gunz.

We reviewed the disappointing previous results in which I had used intra-arterial chemotherapy. We discovered that most of the patients whose head-and-neck cancers I had treated had previously been treated by radiotherapy or surgery or both, and therefore had a compromised blood supply. Such results replicated many times world-wide had given most surgeons the indelible impression that using anti-cancer drugs for these cancers was useless, even if the drugs were infused directly into the artery of supply. This impression then became an entrenched 'article of faith' among almost all doctors who treated cancer, namely that intra-arterial chemotherapy was all but useless.

With the support of Drs Hambly and Gunz I decided to study intra-arterial chemotherapy for advanced cancers that had never been treated previously. This time, however, we would target cancers wherever they occurred as long they had only one artery supplying them which had not been damaged by previous treatment. Compared to the previous results the data now overwhelmingly favoured using intra-arterial chemotherapy as the first in a sequence of available treatments.

I was delighted to discover that my former colleague at 'The Met' in London, Percy Helman, had been appointed Professor of Surgery in Capetown and he was one of the relatively small number of surgeons to adopt this principle. In fact Percy Helman published a paper in the *British Journal of Surgery* in 1968 reporting a great response with huge breast cancers when intra-arterial chemotherapy had been given before other treatment. Either this had not been noticed or had been ignored by Professor Loewenthal.

Unfortunately due to the previous failures in treating localised (single-site) cancers with chemotherapy, the medical establishment remained unconvinced. Only a few centres worldwide adopted a treatment protocol that specified that intra-arterial chemotherapy should be infused into locally-advanced cancers before radiotherapy or surgery was attempted.

Although there was a widespread belief in the failure of preoperative intra-arterial chemotherapy there were still some centres, including my own small unit at Sydney Hospital, that continued to use intra-arterial chemotherapy infused into locally advanced cancers first. In most cases this initial intra-arterial treatment made the cancers significantly smaller so that they could then be eradicated by radiotherapy or by surgery – or by a combination of both.

Encouraged as I was by Drs Dunphy, Hambly, Gunz and later by Professor Milton, I received further encouragement from Sir Howard Florey, later Lord Florey, who was visiting his friend Dr Gunz. Sir Howard, the Australian who first developed penicillin for clinical use, spent a morning with me. He was so interested in our proposal and early findings that he asked me to be sure to keep him informed of our progress. Sadly he died soon after that visit.

Having seen some early responses a number of Sydney Hospital surgeons and other specialists also took a keen interest in my proposal to specialise exclusively in treating previously untreated locally advanced cancers. However for three reasons my immediate plans to establish a specialist Surgical Oncology service had to be put on hold.

Firstly, there was no space in Sydney Hospital to accommodate further development of Surgical Oncology. Secondly, Professor Loewenthal did not support the work. He made it clear that what space was available should be used to develop Professor Milton's Melanoma Unit, and I could not disagree with the need for that. Finally, I was due sabbatical leave and Dr Dunphy had invited me to spend a year as visiting Professor and take part in his research projects in wound healing and organ transplantation. For this I applied for and was awarded a Fulbright Fellowship to the University of California, San Francisco. I realised that a year in San

Francisco would also give me time to complete writing my higher degree MD thesis, 'A Study of Methods of Improving Results of Surgical Management of Potentially Curable Malignant Tumours'.

I therefore decided to defer the battles involved in establishing an independent specialist unit in Surgical Oncology until I had established indisputably strong credentials. As a Fulbright Visiting Professor in one of the world's most prestigious surgical departments I could complete a Doctorate (MD) thesis and prepare a second Masters thesis in surgery (MS) in Dr Dunphy's wound healing laboratory.

By doing this I would have undeniable credentials for establishing a specialist Professorial unit in Surgical Oncology.

On sabbatical in San Francisco

In May 1969 Alison and I and our four small children boarded a plane for San Francisco. On arrival we were met by Bruce Conolly who had been with Dr Dunphy for three years, including a year in a hand-surgery specialist unit in New York. Bruce has subsequently established a first class specialist hand clinic in Sydney Hospital. Bruce and his wife Joyce were about to return to Australia but still found time to meet me and my family. Bruce took us to the apartment he had arranged for us until we found a suitable family house. On the way there he took us to a pancake shop in nearby San Raphael for a meal. The pancake shop made such an impression on our children that for the remainder of our stay in San Francisco they always wanted to be taken there on their birthdays and other special occasions.

We stayed in the apartment for a week while we looked for a house to rent for the year. On the first morning I was swimming in the adjacent swimming pool when I heard a young woman with an obvious Australian accent speaking to her small daughter. We engaged in conversation and learnt that the young woman, Carla, was a nurse from Sydney who had recently become widowed by the sudden death from cerebral haemorrhage of her young doctor husband. From that day Alison and I and our children became firm friends with Carla and Philippa, whom we more-or-less adopted for the year. Towards the end of the year Carla met a young Sydney doctor, Tony Breslin, who had been a friend of her late husband. A mutual attraction developed between them and a year or so later Carla and Tony were married. We have remained good friends ever since.

After a few days Alison and I found a comfortable family home to rent. It was in Corte-Madera (meaning 'cut wood') a San Francisco suburb across the Golden-Gate Bridge in Marin County north of the city. I had to drive across the bridge every day to get to the places where I worked and taught, just as in Sydney I crossed the Sydney Harbour Bridge each day for many years.

The only complication on our first day in the house was the attitude of its canine incumbent. The house owners had two dogs: one a big pure white police-trained German shepherd called Blitz, and the other a small dog of mixed origin. They had arranged accommodation with friends for their smaller dog but planned to leave Blitz in professionally managed kennels for a year. Because I realised how much my family would miss the dog they had left behind in Mosman I offered to care for Blitz during our stay. The owners agreed, but an unforeseen problem arose when I attempted to stride into the backyard to meet and feed Blitz: he threatened to tear me apart. He was very happy to play with the children but being a trained police dog it took some days for me to win his trust and affection. Nevertheless, we gradually became friends.

Blitz was a wonderful dog and assumed the role of protector and friend not only to our family but also our next-door neighbours: a young woman with five young children whose husband was serving in Vietnam. At that time there was also a serial killer targeting children in San Francisco who was known as 'the Zodiac Killer' because of his habit of leaving one of the signs of the Zodiac with his victims' bodies. Our absent neighbour was very grateful for the care Alison and I took of his family – but most especially for the security provided by Blitz.

At Halloween American children customarily knock on people's doors offering them a 'trick or treat' but in 1969 many San Francisco families prevented their children from 'trick or treating' because of fear of the 'Zodiac Killer'. However, in our quiet suburb, largely thanks to Blitz, many children were able to do their 'trick-or-treating'. Another father and I acted as 'bookends' for our small walking party and Blitz patrolled up and down between us, apparently fully aware that his job was to protect the children.

My year in San Francisco was very productive. I worked for six months in Dr Dunphy's wound-healing research lab and six months in Dr Fred Belzer's organ-transplantation lab, and we published several papers together. I continued to do more studies on the healing of wounds and eventually wrote my Master of Surgery thesis on wound-healing.

However, all was not so wonderful on the home front. Alison became unusually friendly with some of our male friends and in particular to one of my work colleagues. Some of my friends hinted to me that something was amiss in our relationship and that I should pay Alison more attention. I tried to ignore the rumours. At the same time I discussed with Dr Dunphy my future plans to specialise exclusively in treating advanced cancers. He was enthusiastic about my project and invited me to consider doing this work in his department in San Francisco. Much as I appreciated his offer I felt my primary obligations were to bring my family back to Australia and with the assurance of the strong support of Colin Hambly and Fred Gunz at Sydney Hospital, I decided I should try to establish a department of Surgical Oncology in Sydney.

I decided that a long family holiday might help to ease the tensions in my family and made plans for us to travel back to Australia via Canada, England, Scotland, Italy, Israel, India and Hong Kong. We arrived back in Sydney in May 1970. Most of our family and friends were struck by the distinct American accents of all of our children, but within three months they were all speaking like Australians again.

Photo of Mum when she became engaged to Dad before he went off to the Great War; Dad shortly before he departed for the war in Europe, 1915.

My much-bandaged Dad in the German hospital for wounded soldiers. He always said that the German doctors and hospital staff treated him as well as they treated their own wounded soldiers and that they saved his life.

The Kurmond Kid aged 3 (left) and 73 (right).

Our little old Kurmond home. (a) Back view taken from the paddock.
(b) Side view taken from the road with my brother, Bruce, holding up the post.

Mum and Dad proudly driving in their new 'T' model Ford, which Dad bought with his army discharge money. Soon Dad had to give up driving, and the car, because of epileptic fits that resulted from his war injuries. Note the solid rubber tyres on motorcars of that vintage.

The last photograph of Dolly, taken at my fifth birthday party. I am at the near end of the table and Dolly is on my right facing the camera. My brother, Bruce, is at the far end, my sister, Evelyn, is partly obscured next to Dolly. The other two girls are neighbourhood friends Virginia and Gaynor Males.

View of the bridge in the Hawkesbury River flood.

Thomson's Ridge Station where I used to catch the train to Richmond school.

The steam locomotive 'Pansy' in March Street Richmond (above), and crossing the Hawkesbury River Bridge (below).

Sunday school outside our home, Kurmond.

The church my parents had built on our property.

Malvern Hill Uniting Church in Croydon, built by my grandfather Frederick Reed and the setting for many family celebrations over several generations, including my parents' wedding.

Running on gas, a war time petrol alternative for motor vehicles

Kurmond School fourth, fifth and sixth classes 1938. I am sixth from the left in the back row.

Kurmond School Reunion, 1970.

Our family photograph taken in about 1941 shortly before Stan turned 18 and enlisted in the RAAF (World War Two). *Back row:* Joyce, Heather, Stan and me. *Front row:* Evelyn, Dad, Elaine, Mum and Bruce.

Horse and cart of Reed and Sons Bakery, owned by my uncles, and a means of earning money in student days.

Graduation day February 1951, with my high school and medical school classmates Len Fienberg (left) and Colin Jennings (right).

A reunion of old mates from Western Suburbs Hospital some thirty years after my year as a senior RMO at that hospital. From left: me, John Sturrock, Bill Doherty, Paul Lush

Off to England as assistant surgeon on board the *Orontes*. It was traditional to farewell family and friends by holding the ends of paper streamers until they broke as the ship moved away from the shore.

At the Pyramids during my time as ship's surgeon.

Lillian

Photograph taken on the tennis court at Wimbledon Hospital with one of the nursing staff. This is the only evidence that I once played tennis at Wimbledon.

With my wife Alison on board the *Queen Elizabeth 1* on our way to America 1960.

Photograph of our children in 1965.
Bobby aged 3, Jenny aged 4, Gillian aged 2 and Peter (front) just a few months old.
Inset: Ten years later one more member of the family, Kate, aged 3.

AN ORGANISATION FOR OUTPATIENT SURGERY

F. O. Stephens
M.B. Sydney, F.R.C.S.E.
LATELY SENIOR SURGICAL REGISTRAR, ABERDEEN ROYAL INFIRMARY *

H. A. F. Dudley
Ch.M. Edin., F.R.C.S.E.
SENIOR LECTURER IN SURGERY, UNIVERSITY OF ABERDEEN

From the Department of Surgery, University of Aberdeen

Many general surgical waiting-lists are so long that a patient with varicose veins or hernia may wait for two or three years to get into hospital. Often such patients are submitted to operation either as outpatients or on a short-stay basis. Farquharson (1955) has described an outpatient organisation designed to treat hernia under local anæsthesia, and he has used the technique on more than 600 patients (Mr. E. L. Farquharson, personal communication). But there is need for a better understanding of the scope and limitations of outpatient surgical treatment, and we here describe the formation of a service in a surgical unit of the Aberdeen Royal Infirmary.

Aberdeen Royal Infirmary is the only large hospital for general surgery in the north-east of Scotland, and the waiting-list of general surgical patients has grown steadily in the past ten years. At the end of 1959 the general waiting-list for the three surgical units (180 beds) was 1600. About a third of the patients on the list of the professorial surgical unit had varicose veins or herniæ. Because of a lengthy list of major surgery these patients had to wait from eighteen months to two years. Increase in beds or staff was not feasible, and it was therefore decided to explore the possibilities of their outpatient treatment by a special team.

* Present address: Department of Surgery, University of Oregon, Portland, Oregon.

The world's first paper on outpatient surgery under general anaesthetic, *The Lancet*, 13 May 1961.

The president of the American College of Surgeons, and the International Colleges of Surgeons, Dr J Englebert Dunphy, (back to camera wearing a grey coat) my friend and mentor, working as a stretcher-bearer in outback Australia!

Mentors and colleagues, supportive of the author's approach to integrated cancer treatment.

Dr Dunphy, President of the American College of Surgeons

Dr Bill Larkins, Secretary of the AMA

Dr John Bain, first doctor in Kurmond Kurrajong district

Dr Colin Hambly, radiotherapist

Dr Fred Gunz, haematologist and Director of Research

The distinguished Lord Florey of penicillin fame

Cutting the ribbon at the entrance of 'Fred's shed' (the first independent surgical oncology unit in Australia) on its opening day in 1980. On my right are Dr Will Hanks and Sister Vickie Saker. On my left are Sister Libby Kimmorley and Sister Amy Teoh.

Oncology nurses who were essential to the success of surgical oncology, integrated treatments in my Sydney Hospital and Royal Prince Alfred Hospital Units (above, and following page).
Janine Bell (left) and Leanne Watson; Amy Teoh is the photo at top.

Oncology nurses

Jenny Dempsey

Rosemary Farrell

Gabrielle Prest

Cheryl Daley

The Sydney Morning Herald

FIRST PUBLISHED 1831

Cancer team's drug alternative

By SHAUN McILRAITH

A Sydney cancer team is so encouraged by the results of treating breast cancer with drugs that it has proposed it as an alternative for women who object to mastectomy, the surgical removal of a breast.

The treatment advanced by the team is to attack the cancer with drugs sent straight to it through the bloodstream, then follow up with radiotherapy.

Members of the team believe their results in treating seven cases of advanced, inoperable breast cancer by this method justify offering it to women with earlier cancers who are strongly against losing a breast.

They make the suggestion in a report, published today in the British journal, The Lancet, on the first four patients to receive the drug treatment and radiotherapy for advanced breast cancer. The drug treatment is known as chemotherapy.

Professor STEPHENS

The team is led by Professor Frederick O. Stephens, an associate professor of surgery at Sydney University.

He and his colleagues at Sydney Hospital are one of a very few teams in the world — possibly no more than three — to have used chemotherapy and radiotherapy as an initial treatment for breast cancer.

Like many other cancer specialists around the world, Professor Stephens has been using chemotherapy for several years to make large tumours shrink so that subsequent surgery or radiotherapy can be more successful.

The drugs are directed straight to the target by infusing them through a tube in an artery supplying blood to the tumour area.

Earlier, a blue dye is released into the artery to confirm by its discolouration of the skin that the drugs will reach the right place.

In his use of the methods Professor Stephens has concentrated in the last 10 years on people with large tumours who have had no previous treatment for their cancer.

One of the team said yesterday he had concluded that indifferent results with arterial chemotherapy in other parts of the world were due to the effects of previous radiotherapy or surgery on the blood supply to a tumour.

Both impaired the blood vessel system around a tumour with the result that the amount of drug reaching the cancer was greatly reduced.

Their initial-treatment chemotherapy for advanced breast cancer differs from that of other teams in that he uses four different anti-cancer drugs in combination, instead of one or two.

The drugs — 5-fluorouracil, vincristine, methotrexate and adriamycin — attack cells at different stages of division. Cancer cells are more vulnerable to the attack as they divide more often than normal cells.

The seven women with advanced breast cancer have been treated by Professor Stephens and the team in the last four years. Six have survived without apparent recurrence of the disease.

The first patient, a 55-year-old woman who had an erupting cancer occupying most of her right breast, is still alive with two apparently healthy breasts. She plays golf regularly.

Before and after photographs of the women show that the treatment has completely reduced big, open cancers, which in one case engulfed the whole breast.

One patient, a 45-year-old woman whose right breast returned to normal after treatment, developed a small tumour in the other breast about a year later.

Although mastectomy was recommended, she insisted on having the same treatment again. The second tumour disappeared, leaving an apparently healthy breast.

Professor Stephens does not claim the treatment is a cure for cancer and, in fact, the woman who died relapsed because of a secondary growth elsewhere in the body.

However, he does regard it as effective in controlling cancer in the breast.

"My contention is that because such advanced cancers respond so well with this plan of management, we should consider offering it to patients with less advanced cancer who have an abhorrence of losing a breast," he said.

"I think we have enough information to say we have a reasonable alternative for these women."

"But I don't think we know enough about the treatment to offer it to all patients."

Front page, *Sydney Morning Herald,* 30 August 1980.

After my third 'City to Surf' run. It was the first run for my daughters Jenny (left) and Katie (right).

Sheilagh and I exchange wedding rings in the historic St David's church at Kurrajong Heights. Reverend Helen Anderson officiated.

Colleagues in cancer research

Dr (later Professor) Bill Marsden

Professor Richard Fox

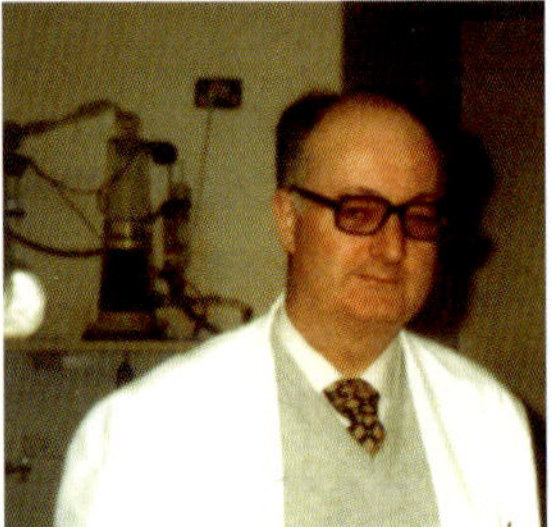

Dr Frank Neil

Dr Stan McCarthy

Members of the Department of Surgery after I had been appointed Head of the department in 1987.
Front row: Professor Les Bokay, Professor Gerry Milton, myself, Professor Tom Reeve and Professor Bob Lusby. Behind Les Bokay are Professor John Harris, Dr Paul Satchell and Miss Tessa Milne. Behind my right shoulder is Dr Peter Gosch and behind my left shoulder is Professor Tim Cartmill. *Back row from left:* Professor Bill McCarthy, Associate Professor Peter Thursby, Associate Professor Pierre Chapuis, Professor Bill Gibson, Associate Professor Janet McCreadie, Associate Professor Ross Smith, Professor John Thompson and Professor John Fletcher.

Sheilagh and I celebrating my election as the first president of The International Society for Regional Cancer Therapy. On my right is Professor Karl Aigner from Wiesbaden, Germany, who nominated me for the position and (far left) Professor Ed Krementz of New Orleans.

Dr Professor Karl Aigner (Charlie) founder of the International Society for Regional Cancer Therapy being congratulated by Pope John-Paul II in recognition of his contributions to surgical oncology.

Six of the world's most respected surgical oncologists at a meeting in Germany. *From left:* myself, Professor Ferdy Lejeune (Switzerland), Professor Prabir K Chaudhuri (USA), Professor Ed Krementz (USA, the 'father' of surgical oncology), Professor Alexander Eggermont (Holland), Professor Karl Aigner (Germany and Professor Herman Schraffordt-Koops (Holland).

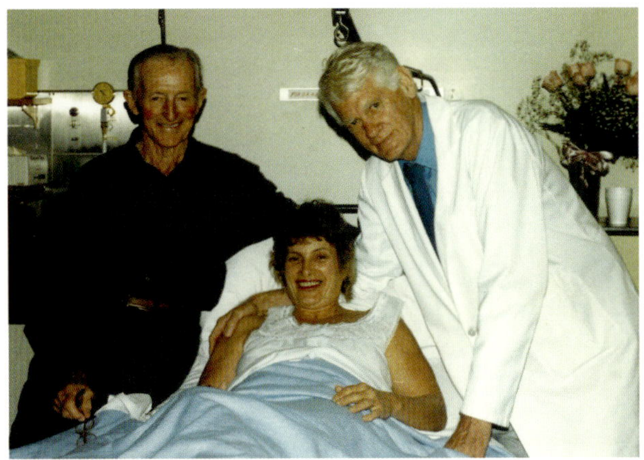

With Alan Somerville and Patricia Fordham. Alan who had avoided a total limb and buttock amputation for a large cancer 7 years previously was giving encouragement to Pat who was being treated with an implanted chemotherapy infusion pump in her abdominal wall for metastatic liver cancers.

Beneath the 'Tree of Hippocrates', on the isle of Kos, Greece.

Chapter Four

Specialising in Cancer Surgery

After returning from America early in 1970 I re-established my work in Sydney Hospital and continued to get much better results in treating locally advanced cancers. Many patients were referred to me by my Sydney Hospital surgical, medical and other specialist colleagues and I gradually received some direct referrals from doctors who practised elsewhere. Unfortunately the notion that chemotherapy had no place in treating locally advanced cancers was still widely held by most surgeons outside of Sydney Hospital.

Because there was no space for a separate cancer clinic in the hospital I continued to do most of my clinic work in the radiotherapy department through the co-operation and good grace of Colin Hambly and his staff. Eventually, with the support of Colin Hambly, Fred Gunz and the medical superintendent, the Sydney Hospital Board agreed to buy a caravan and set up clinic facilities attached to the radiotherapy service. This was known as The Surgical Cancer Clinic or, within the hospital 'Fred's Shed'. I believe it was not only the first independent Surgical Oncology clinic in Australia but may even have predated the establishment of any independent Australian Medical Oncology clinic as a separate entity.

The AMA secretary, Bill Larkins, was so impressed with the success we were having at Sydney Hospital that he arranged for me to visit a number of country hospitals to speak about my work and the results we were achieving. I initially accompanied two distinguished senior specialists, Dr Harry Kramer (Pathologist) and Dr Kelvin McGarrity (Gynaecologist) on their visits to country hospitals. Bill also helped arrange for me to spend two weeks as the 'Bay of Plenty Visiting Professor' in New Zealand in 1972, a week in Melbourne University's hospital in Geelong in 1977, and a week in 1983 as Visiting Professor in Adelaide University's Teaching Hospital, the Queen Elizabeth Hospital.

Six years later, after he had established his new Orthopaedic Department in Queensland, Professor Bill Marsden invited me for a week as his first Visiting Professor in the Royal Brisbane Hospital.

While I was pleased to speak of my work on all of these occasions I was unable to demonstrate the techniques on patients because it would have required much more than a week or two's visit. To initiate treatment and then not to be able to follow through with the level of supervision, care and professional co-operation required for five or six weeks was fraught with difficulty, and was certainly not in the best interests of the patient in the event of something going wrong.

Surgical oncology: early protagonists and antagonists

Dr Dunphy invited me back to America on three occasions to speak about my work in surgical oncology and he continued to encourage our studies until his death in 1981. He was a protagonist of combined clinics involving the disciplines of surgery, chemotherapy and radiotherapy. I was disappointed not to be able to accept his invitations to accept a Chair of Surgery in a new hospital in Portland and later to develop surgical oncology in San Francisco. I had to tell him that I wanted to raise our children in the more peaceful living conditions in Australia, even though the facilities and financial rewards and prospects of developing surgical oncology as a specialty in America would have been much greater.

It was always a disappointment to me that in Sydney neither Professor Loewenthal, nor the two subsequent Deans of Medicine at Sydney University nor even the Foundation Professor of Medical Oncology showed any interest in seeing first-hand what we were achieving with our integrated treatment for advanced cancers. The accumulation of papers from our unit that were being published in local and overseas medical and surgical journals seemed to have no impact on the Australian authorities who could have done most to provide facilities for further studies and treatment.

Professor Loewenthal's prominence as a leading Australian surgeon and his pre-eminence as Dean of the Faculty of Medicine at the University of Sydney and President of the Royal Australasian College of Surgeons gave credibility to his negative views about surgical oncology. His position was therefore widely accepted as gospel both in Australia and in several other countries where he was well known. He had not had success with pre-operative chemotherapy even given by intra-arterial infusion, and therefore he would not accept that any other surgeon could have success.

Despite these frustrations my years in Sydney Hospital were very happy and productive. With very limited space and facilities I established an active surgical oncology unit, although that title had not at the time been invented to describe the work we were doing. My unit was strongly supported by members of the hospital staff and administration, especially by Dr Hambly and Professor Gunz. However, when the opportunity presented for the appointment of a professor in the field of oncology, John Loewenthal decided not to appoint a Professor of Surgical Oncology at Sydney Hospital but instead he supported the appointment of an overseas candidate nominated by the Ludwig Foundation to a Foundation Chair of Medical Oncology at the Royal Prince Alfred Hospital. He had wanted this to be under his direction but the overseas Professor who was selected by the Ludwig Foundation became a member of the Department of Medicine at the Royal Prince Alfred Hospital. During the political manoeuvring that followed, the Ludwig Foundation transferred its funding for the chair to Melbourne University.

Establishing the Clinical Oncology Society of Australia – COSA

In 1970 Dr Lester Atkinson, a highly respected radiotherapist from the University of New South Wales, invited Professor Milton and me to meet with him at the Prince of Wales Hospital to discuss forming an inter-university cancer specialist group. At Lester's suggestion we agreed to have regular meetings and our group was joined by surgeons Dr Todd Davis and Dr Michael Donellan and later by radiotherapist Dr Lester Peters.

At Lester Atkinson's suggestion we agreed to call this group the Clinical Oncology Society of Australia, later to be known as COSA. In the same period some general physicians, led by haematologists, developed an increasing interest in using chemotherapy to treat widespread cancer. As newer anti-cancer drugs became available, increasing numbers of general physicians took a special interest in cancer treatment. Many specialised exclusively in cancer treatment with chemotherapy and became known as medical oncologists. Some then assumed that if any chemotherapy was to be used in the treatment of advanced cancers they should be in charge of such patients, and invite surgeons and radiotherapists when their help was needed.

The first Sydney specialists in medical oncology resented a surgeon adopting the name 'Surgical Oncologist'. The attitude of the early medical oncology specialists was that the use of the new chemotherapeutic agents was their special equipment and should not be used by a surgeon any more than a scalpel and other operating equipment should be used by a specialist physician. Professor Loewenthal accepted this attitude and encouraged appointments of medical oncologists trained to use the increasing numbers of anticancer drugs with different biological actions, and to establish more cancer departments headed by medical oncologists. A number of medical oncologists were invited to join COSA and within a few years, by sheer dint of numbers, they were the association's dominant professional group. Similar chemotherapy specialisation had developed worldwide so that medical oncologists rapidly became an important worldwide specialty group.

My special interest in chemotherapy was to use it to reduce the size and activity of locally advanced cancers to make them more curable by a following surgical operation – but for some time this aspect was not recognised by the growing community of medical oncologists. When eventually it was recognised they labelled it with a new name '*neoadjuvant*' a mixture of Greek and Latin; *neo* being Greek for 'new' and *adjuvant* being Latin for 'assistant'. They were wrong on both counts. Not only did this manufactured word bastardise and confuse Greek and Latin, but, the process was not new. Professor Ed Krementz in New Orleans, Professor Percy Helman in South Africa, Professor L.B.M. Joseph in the Christian Medical College in Vellore, India, and several other surgeons in different parts of the world including myself had been using chemotherapy to reduce cancers before operation for several years.

In Australia the newly appointed medical oncologists assumed that surgeons had no role to play in the use of anti-cancer drugs and that surgical use of intra-arterial chemotherapy had been proven to be of little, if any, value. Most surgeons, including Professor Loewenthal, were satisfied with the reasoning that if a cancer could not be cured by surgery alone, someone else should have responsibility for the patient.

Professor Loewenthal encouraged the appointment of numerous medical oncologists as well as the establishment of cancer departments headed by this specialty. He believed that any well-trained surgeon could perform cancer surgery when needed so that there was no need for the specialty of surgical oncology.

Despite all this my conviction about the efficacy of using pre-operative chemotherapy for difficult/more advanced local cancers was not diminished. While the number of cases would be relatively small in our population, I believed that it could and should form part of an integrated approach to the management and cure of such cancers. However I was to experience a lot more frustration and disappointment as I persevered in this direction.

Career choice – between a rock and a hard place

The absence of consensus within the medical fraternity and the competing demands of state government and hospital services in the expanding Western Sydney area contributed to a situation where I was faced with a career choice: to develop a Surgical Oncology Unit in an overcrowded Sydney Hospital or to accept a Chair of Surgery elsewhere.

Sydney Hospital had been battling for years to be rebuilt either on its present site or somewhere nearby. I became involved in the negotiations around this following my appointment in 1972 as a member of the Sydney Hospital board.

At the time my cousin Stan Stephens was a Minister in the New South Wales government, and all agreed that this connection could help in the negotiations between the hospital, the university and the government. Stan, who was Minister for Housing, introduced me to the then Minister for Health, Harry Jago. I subsequently tried to help mediate between the Hospital (with its President Dr Frank Ritchie), and the University of Sydney (with Professor John Loewenthal) in negotiations to redevelop Sydney Hospital.

When the State government changed hands Harry Jago introduced me to the new minister, Kevin Stewart. (While Harry Jago and Kevin Stewart were political opponents they were friends in private.) I soon found that gaining agreement between the Conservative and Labor sides of politics proved considerably easier than effecting agreement between the hospital and university institutional heads who remained bitter rivals. But after discussing several possible sites for a new Sydney Hospital the state government made an offer of a site at Westmead, 23 km west of Sydney. I was convinced that the Westmead site should be accepted because I believed it would be Sydney Hospital's only realistic chance to acquire new and updated premises for its highly skilled clinical, teaching, and research activities and staff.

I was always supported in these deliberations by my Sydney Hospital medical academic colleague Associate Professor Sol Posen. By then Sol had also been appointed to the hospital board and he maintained just as strongly as I that if Sydney Hospital was to be rebuilt the only realistic opportunity would be Westmead. We were supported by another astute member of the hospital board, Mr Les Hooker, founder of the LJ Hooker real estate empire. However, Dr Ritchie remained adamant that he would not accept a Sydney Hospital so far away from the city. He persuaded the hospital board to reject the offer. He postulated that a new teaching hospital was needed in the central city region so it would have to be where the skilled and experienced Sydney Hospital staff wanted it to be.

Although he had initially opposed the idea of a teaching hospital so far away from the university, the rejection of the proposal by the Sydney Hospital Board cleared the way for John Loewenthal to take an interest in building a new university hospital at Westmead – independent of his rivals at Sydney Hospital. Before his Westmead hospital plan was even agreed to by the state government, Professor Loewenthal suggested that I should drop all contact with Sydney Hospital and join the staff of the old hospital at Parramatta near Westmead where I could establish a general Professorial surgical unit in readiness for the move to Westmead.

I declined because it would have meant giving up all association with Sydney Hospital and my continuing hope for its relocation to Westmead. The minister, Kevin Stewart, offered a compromise-proposal for a gradual transfer of Sydney Hospital from the centre of

Sydney to the new site at Westmead over 15 years. I was even more concerned that if I moved independently to Parramatta it would also mean giving up my work in surgical oncology, which I considered vital.

Surgical oncology could not be established in Parramatta Hospital because it had no readily available radiotherapy, haematology or pathology services and it would not have these until a proposed new Westmead Hospital was built. I felt that my priority was to stay put and try to continue developing surgical oncology even though it could mean losing my best opportunity for a full Chair with a department of surgical oncology. On the other hand, I realised that having me established in the old Parramatta Hospital and then in his planned new Westmead Hospital would solve two of John Loewenthal's objectives. First it would get me away from his Sydney Hospital rivals and it would also stop me from promoting my 'crazy' idea of establishing surgical oncology as a specialisation. My assessment of the situation proved to be accurate. Choosing to stay at Sydney Hospital in order to continue developing surgical oncology was regarded as an act of defiance. I should have realised that this would be my last chance of receiving Professor Loewenthal's support to secure a Chair of Surgery. The choice being offered was to either give up my special interest in surgical oncology or relinquish any hope of having his support for a chair.

John Loewenthal expanded and built a great University Department of Surgery but only in areas that had been shown to be feasible in overseas studies. He had no interest or insight into new or unproven concepts that required pioneering dedication and work – and it turned out my experience with him was not unique. Sydney's renowned pioneer in microsurgery Dr Earl Owen, had had a similar experience. Dr Owen had developed a special interest in microsurgery and using its techniques in 1970 he re-attached the severed finger of a child. His immediate superior did not believe microsurgical re-attachment was possible and had declined permission for the operation to proceed. When it was reported to Professor Loewenthal that Dr Owen had proceeded with the operation without permission he was dismissed for insubordination. Later, after the operation had proven successful, Dr Owen went on to become the world's first Professor of Microsurgery in another university.

Subsequently another bright young research/lecturer in our department, Dr Milton Waner, now Professor Milton Waner of the Beth-Israel Institute in New York, received similar treatment. Professor Loewenthal did not accept that Milton Waner was getting the results he claimed in using photodynamic treatment of early mouth and skin cancers or in treating visible vascular lesions in or under the skin. Milton Waner was dismissed but he was subsequently appointed Professor and Director of Vascular and Birthmarks Institutes first in Arkansas, and later in New York.

Sydney Hospital: the end of an era

The early 1970s were a time of expanding university funding, so deans of medical schools, and to some extent heads of departments, had the authority to do things as never before or since. In Professor Loewenthal's case, his pre-eminence in the Australian Medical establishment led to his being able to wield near dictatorial authority in administrative circles. Those who offered dissenting opinions were regarded as both wrong and disloyal.

Eventually under his leadership a grand new hospital was built at Westmead, staffed, not by Sydney Hospital clinicians, researchers and teachers, but by people whom Professor Loewenthal considered both able and loyal. Subsequently Sydney Hospital was reduced in size and importance and stripped of its function as a major teaching hospital. Major specialist departments, including the great Kanematsu Research Institute and the Melanoma Unit, were transferred to one or other of Sydney's remaining teaching hospitals and the radiotherapy department was dismantled. The then New South Wales Labor Health Minister and his colleagues should hang their heads in shame. It was all the more disappointing to me personally because despite an introduction to the minister by my friend Paul Keating, then a shadow minister in the federal government, and after what I thought was an agreed compromise proposal, the end result was that Sydney Hospital became a relatively small and minor teaching hospital attached to a specialist eye hospital.

The prolonged dispute to save the hospital as a major teaching hospital came to an end in 1983 and resulted in a major disruption to hospital services. The Minister of Health decided that by closing the hospital he could save money and make its valuable site available for the expansion of facilities for politicians in the adjacent NSW Parliament House. His plan lacked any apparent concern for the quality of care and quality of the staff, the history, or the convenience of Sydney Hospital to people throughout the state, country and city. There was, however, so much public protest at the planned closure that the minister's plan to destroy it was eventually modified to a reduction in the hospital's services. But this still involved it losing its status as a major teaching hospital. Medical students and university academics were to be moved to the state's closest remaining general teaching hospitals: Royal Prince Alfred, Royal North Shore, St Vincent's, and Prince of Wales, and two or three specialists were relocated to the new Westmead Hospital.

Despite its significance in Australia's social and political history the hospital was downgraded to predominantly become an eye hospital with a small general hospital attached. Its proud history included the following: it was Australia's first school of nursing, established under the auspices of Florence Nightingale and her trainee, Lucy Osborne. It became Australia's first teaching hospital in 1814 when it enrolled Australia's first medical student. (From that time it had become responsible for training about ten per cent of Australia's practising doctors, including many specialists.) It was Australia's first hospital to use a stethoscope (1850), and chloroform general anaesthetic (1862). It was the strike disaster hospital for waterfront and marine disasters, including the victims of the Japanese mini-submarine torpedo attacks of World War II. Other notable firsts for the hospital had been coronary care (Dr Desmond Julian), the first report of renal damage caused by APC powders (Dr Lionel Jacobs), and renal dialysis (Drs John Mahony and John Stewart).

The closure of Sydney Hospital as a major teaching hospital, the loss of Fred Gunz and the Kanematsu research with its haematology and all embracing pathology services, and especially, the loss of Colin Hambly and the radiotherapy service at Sydney Hospital, resulted in the disbanding of Australia's first service devoted specifically to surgical oncology.

Because the hospital was no longer to have radiotherapy, or specialist pathology or an appropriate ward or other essential facilities, I had to move my unit to give it any chance of survival. But by this time medical oncologists had been appointed to take charge of specialist cancer services in all other teaching hospitals. It was a common view that an independent service in surgical oncology might be seen as a competing service to the newly established services in medical oncology, and as such it was not warmly welcomed.

I chose to move my unit to the Royal Prince Alfred Hospital (RPAH) where I had worked as a senior lecturer in surgery 20 years previously. I still had a number of friends at RPAH and some rooms in an old nurses' home were allocated for my unit; but I really had to start from scratch with minimal facilities.

RPAH's major cancer services were under the care of medical oncologists, and I knew, without a full department with an independent professor it was going to be difficult to build up a unit again. However, I decided that I must try.

It is worth noting that in 1995 the Royal Alexandra Children's Hospital at Camperdown, which was in a run-down condition, faced a similar dilemma to the one faced by Sydney Hospital. However its medical staff had learned from Sydney's experience and recommended that the directors of the hospital should accept an invitation to re-establish the hospital at Westmead.

Surgical oncology wonders

Despite all of the obstacles in my path I continued developing my special interest in the treatment of locally advanced cancers and I experienced great satisfaction from the growing number of better-than-expected results for patients who had previously been considered incurable or curable only by radical mutilating surgery such as amputation of a limb.

I gave up general surgical practice (except when I was on emergency duty) and concentrated on 'integrated cancer treatment' for locally advanced cancers. The most taxing difficulty with this work was that each patient receiving intra-arterial chemotherapy required constant supervision day and night for up to five or even six weeks. The special nurse working with me, and also the ward charge nurse, learned what to do if attention was needed and I always made myself available at home or by telephone in case something unusual needed to be addressed. Being the only qualified surgeon doing this work I was on call twenty-four hours a day, seven days a week but when my help was needed the problem could usually be sorted fairly quickly.

If it wasn't for the interest and support of Professors Gerry Milton, Bill McCarthy and later John Thompson, who were at the time establishing their world-renowned melanoma unit I would not have been able to arrange for any holiday breaks with my family. Later, with the assistance of these same people, I was able to accept a number of overseas invitations to speak of my work.

I am also indebted to a series of excellent oncology nurses who became the backbone of my patient-care programs. Constant supervision is needed in oncology regimens, especially when intra-arterial chemotherapy is used. The correct flow of drugs must be maintained over some weeks while ensuring the drugs are concentrating and destroying cells in the cancer and not destroying healthy tissues in a nearby region. I feel sure that the main reason this work has not been widely practised is because too many people who have tried it have made mistakes that can be avoided only by constant skilled supervision over a period of up to six weeks. Over the years Sue Cruickshank, Jenny Dempsey, Amy Teoh, Rosemary Farrell, Gabrielle Priest, Jenene Bell, Leanne Watson and Cheryl Daley became so skilled and reliable in detecting problems that I came to depend on them for the success of our work.

Chapter Five

Special Memories of Sydney Hospital

Cyclone Tracy

We were only remotely involved with the damage done by Cyclone Tracy to the city of Darwin on Christmas Eve 1974. Hospitals in or near Darwin that had not been destroyed by the cyclone were full to overflowing, so like other major Australian hospitals, Sydney Hospital took some patients injured by the cyclone and some patients who had been in hospitals that had been destroyed by Cyclone Tracy. I had only one such patient, a man with an advanced cancer of his face that had destroyed much of one side of his nose. He had been treated successfully by radiotherapy and had been admitted to Darwin hospital in preparation for plastic surgery but declined to have surgery in Sydney, preferring to defer the surgery and return to Darwin to help his family.

The Granville Railway Disaster

I became much more involved in treating victims of the Granville train disaster. Early on the morning of 18 January 1977, I happened to be listening to the radio when I heard that a train travelling from Mount Victoria to Sydney had left the rails and crashed into a bridge at Granville. I was particularly concerned because I knew that my brother, Bruce, and members of his family sometimes travelled on that train. I phoned the hospital superintendent who alerted the hospital disaster-response emergency team and then drove to Granville where one of the Sydney Hospital team, Dr Jim Ellis, was already in action. He took me through the tunnel under the huge concrete slabs to see what had happened. It was a most horrific scene, the like of which I hope I will never see again. Huge concrete slabs and blocks had crashed onto the train crushing people in their seats. Most were dead but some were still alive and badly in need of help.

The busy emergency and ambulance teams had already removed those who could be removed but others remained trapped until the concrete slabs could be moved. Some passengers survived while others who were removed died either before anything could be done to help them or soon after being admitted to a hospital. Eighty-three people were killed but no-one who was there was left untouched. I was reassured that none of my brother's family was on that train.

I have sad memories of one particular young man who had one leg and thigh crushed between two huge concrete blocks. Dr Ellis and I did what we could for him but until a crane was able to move one of the concrete blocks he could not be released. Otherwise he appeared well and chatted to us freely. When he was eventually released we had to decide whether we should amputate his limb on the spot. Evidence from similar 'crush injuries' during the London air raids in World War II indicated that people with such 'crush injuries' would die from what was called 'crush syndrome' unless the limb was amputated. However, as a helicopter was readily available to take him to a hospital with a major trauma unit we decided not to perform what would have been a crude amputation with very limited equipment in an open, unclean environment. It was suggested that with modern emergency care and kidney dialysis facilities the man should survive without a crude amputation. However, even though he was airlifted by helicopter to a major trauma unit for immediate care we were saddened to learn that he died from 'crush syndrome' a day or two later.

But there were also some less tragic stories from that era. Many doctors at Sydney Hospital also had, and still have, a wonderful tradition of helping to teach and promote good health practices in disadvantaged countries, largely at their own expense. Among these were Bruce and Joyce Conolly, Orthopaedic Surgeons, the late Jim Ellis, Don Faithful and Bill Bye, and the Professor of Ophthalmology, Frank Billson.

Other memorable incidents

Matchmaker

One year I had a very good unmarried registrar assistant from Singapore. At the same time in my new fourth year student group I noticed a beautiful young female student who also happened to come from Singapore. I asked the registrar if he had met her and described her thus: 'She is just gorgeous, pretty dumb mind you, but lovely to look at'. The registrar explained that he had indeed met the young lady in question and that she was in fact his fiancée!

In spite of my indiscretion we have all remained good friends ever since. The truth is that she is very bright but rather reserved. However, when they later took me to dinner when I visited Singapore some years later she was not too reserved to remind me of the incident.

The absent-minded professor

One story I will never forget concerns one of my professorial friends whom some considered to be the original absent-minded professor. This professor was known for his good work helping the sick in undeveloped countries. One night at 9pm his wife phoned the hospital to ask why her husband had not yet come home for dinner. His dinner had been ready for a couple of hours. His assistant replied: 'Didn't he tell you that he was going to spend a couple of weeks in Bangladesh?'

Professors can be dumb too

Professors and even associate professors are supposed to know everything but there are times when we look particularly dumb. On one occasion I was worried about my son, Peter. When he was two years old he developed a constant discharge from his nose, but from only one nostril. Thinking of all the nasty polyps and other even worse nasties that can be responsible for such a nasal discharge I phoned my friend Dr Bruce Benjamin (paediatric ENT specialist) to ask if he would kindly see my son rather urgently. 'I will', Bruce said, 'but have you looked for an apple-core or something up his nose?' I had not done this. Sure enough there was half an apple-core stuck high up his nostril. I removed it with a pair of forceps, achieving an immediate cure. When I told Bruce he laughed and has since reminded me of my lack of diagnostic skills.

Father confessor

During my years at Sydney Hospital I had a series of both male and female junior resident doctors and trainee surgical registrars working in my unit who were all intelligent, amiable and enthusiastic. Some are now leading specialists in different fields of medicine as well as surgery, and one or two have become successful medical administrators. I still keep in touch with many of those who have settled in Sydney and some have become close friends.

Often a junior doctor in my team would ask for advice about various matters, most often about their future careers and career choices, but sometimes about social matters or affairs of the heart. The most unusual of these experiences was with Hari Kapila, my surgical registrar at the time, who was originally from India. Hari had been in Perth and other parts of Australia for some years and at Sydney Hospital for about a year before he joined my team. By his own assessment he had become quite Australianised socially. He enjoyed parties, watched and participated in various sporting activities and had been altogether thoroughly enjoying his newfound Australian way of life. But suddenly he had received a letter from his father in India saying that a bride had been chosen for him and that he should return to India to get married. He was totally confused. He loved and respected his parents but he only vaguely remembered meeting the young lady his family had chosen for him. He simply did not know her. He was reluctant not to obey his father, a highly regarded high-caste doctor whom he knew would have been insulted and publicly humiliated by a refusal.

Hari and I chatted for some time before I finally advised him that since Indian marriages seemed to be more stable and happier than Australian marriages, perhaps his father might be more likely to have made a better choice of bride than Hari would himself. I suggested that at least he should return to India meet the young lady and that they should assess for themselves the pros and cons of marriage. I also said that the young lady was probably just as apprehensive as he was.

Hari duly returned to India, met the young lady and realised what a good choice his father had made. He then brought his new bride back to Sydney where he continued to work and study. He is now a leading specialist in hand surgery and microsurgery and lives happily in Sydney with his lovely wife Kirti who is also a doctor. They now have three lovely children all of whom are also doctors.

A special box of wine

One clinical event in my life causes some people to laugh and dedicated wine-lovers to cry. In Portland with Dr Dunphy I had made some special studies of bile duct function and methods of repair and had published a paper on this subject. Not long after my appointment at Sydney Hospital a surgeon in another hospital had made a potentially lethal mistake. In removing a patient's gallbladder he had accidentally removed a section of her bile duct. Without prompt repair of the bile duct the patient would have died. The surgeon had heard of my work and interest in bile duct repairs so he sent the patient to be admitted under my care at Sydney Hospital.

I was able to repair the damage and the patient made a full recovery. Shortly thereafter I found a box of red wine on our doorstep with a letter of gratitude from the surgeon involved. Neither Alison nor I were wine drinkers but Alison knew how to make a good stew and a good wine trifle so we used the wine in stews and trifles and found it also improved the flavour of tomato soup. We did taste some ourselves and thought it tasted OK on its own. But one evening we invited some friends for dinner and served them some of the wine. Our friends asked what the special occasion was. I said that there was no special occasion that it was just that we had two bottles of wine left from a box of twelve we had been given, and thought they might like some. If our friends were incredulous about our ignorance of the value of Grange Hermitage (Australia's most famous wine) they were utterly horrified when we told them that we had used most of the other bottles in stews, soups and trifles!

Andie

I had worked as a surgeon for ten years at Sydney Hospital with an excellent operating theatre sister, Sister Anderson-Stuart, nicknamed Andie. When I was operating Andie always knew exactly what instrument I needed next. I did not even have to know the name of the instrument, all that was required was for me to put out my hand and Andie would place the appropriate instrument into it for my next move. I was in awe of her intuition until one day when I had not noticed that she was supervising a trainee nurse. Having my eye focused on a small bleeding point deep in a large abdomen I held out my hand expecting it to be filled with the appropriate instrument but nothing happened. I waited several seconds and suddenly I heard Andie's voice call out; 'Put something into his bloody hand nurse! He'll use it, it doesn't matter what it is'!

A legal faux pas

Somewhat reluctantly I have one more classic Stephens booboo to confess. Some years ago as a newcomer at Sydney Hospital my Australian mentor and friend Dr Bill Larkins invited Alison and me to dinner. He did not tell us who the other guests were to be but when we arrived he introduced the two other guests thus: 'Fred and Alison Stephens I would like you to meet Tony and Patricia Mason. In reality they are Sir Anthony and Lady Patricia'. They were a pleasant youngish couple not much older than us. Believing that Bill was my pulling my leg as he was wont to do I shook their hands and said: 'Pleased to meet you Tony and Pat. I am Sir Frederick and this is Lady Alison but you can just call us Fred and Alison'. They laughed. It was in fact Sir Anthony Mason, Chief Justice of the High Court of Australia and his wife!

Chapter Six

Big Changes on the Home Front

In 1971 Alison became pregnant but tragically miscarried. We were both very saddened by this because we had wanted just one more baby, however Alison soon fell pregnant again with our daughter Katriona. We had agreed on the baby's name but I got into trouble when I mistakenly wrote Katriona instead of Catriona on the birth certificate. I had thought Katriona was the spelling of the Scottish name that Alison wanted. I was later forgiven when we came across the name of a woman in a remote Scottish Highland village who spelled her name with a 'K'.

I was also in trouble for missing the baby's birth. Sydney Hospital has never had an obstetrics unit so Alison was booked into the Crown Street Women's Hospital two or three kilometres away. When Alison's labour began I arranged with friends who understood my work to stand by so that I could be at the birth. For four days they duly covered my duties but during the fifth I had an emergency call from the hospital that I had to attend to personally. Of course during my brief three-hour absence, beautiful golden-haired Katriona – now called Kate – decided to say hello to the world without me being present.

Our growing family needed more space so Alison and I decided to have an upper storey built onto our house. This took all the finance we could muster but our 'Cape Cod' top storey was – and remains – a great success. We now had plenty of room for our children and a beautiful harbour view. All was well with the Stephens family.

Apart from my work we spent all our time together as a family. My family loved Alison and the children and we often visited them and socialised with our hospital, university, school, kindergarten and Sunday school friends and their families.

From 1970 onwards I was usually able to arrange admission of patients at convenient times to allow Alison and me to take our kids on holidays twice a year. Every year we made a point of taking one week's holiday with some friends and their children in a holiday camp in Bundanoon in the Southern Highlands south-west of Sydney. We stayed in a rambling old boarding house called 'Rosnell'. On other school holidays our family, and two of our closest companion families, the McClures and the Simeons, took camping or caravan holidays in a caravan park on the Manning River about 350 km north of Sydney. But soon after our Manning River holiday in January 1973, when Katie was only four months old, Alison became particularly close to another school mother, a young woman with three schoolchildren whom everyone, except her husband, knew was having an affair with a young school-teacher. As Alison's friendship with this woman deepened and Alison began spending more time with her, I began to worry. I had to attend a surgical meeting in Perth and when I returned my next-door neighbour suggested I should be careful of leaving Alison for long periods. He said she was not only seeing a great deal of her lady friend from school but seemed to have struck up a more-than-close friendship with a young man from up the road.

My concern was compounded when on one occasion I visited the McClure's home to find Alison there smoking a cigarette. I hit the roof. She was certainly taken aback as I don't think I had ever been angry with her before. She had never, to my knowledge, been a smoker. She knew how I detested smoking and that especially as a cancer surgeon, I was horrified at the example she would set for my patients and our five beautiful children. Even in 1973 it was obvious that smoking was responsible for most of the most serious mouth and throat cancers that I was treating.

Our children are devastated

It was as a result of that chance discovery that I realised something was wrong with our marriage. Some days later Alison announced that she was leaving me – and the children. Our baby was just one year old. I begged her not to leave saying that if she insisted on ending our marriage she should stay at home and I would leave.

She refused and stated that she did not want to be 'saddled with five kids'. I was sure that her 'friend' from the children's school had convinced her that 'there was a lot of fun to be had out there' and that she was missing out on it all.

We discussed Alison's desire to leave with the children. They all pleaded with her not to go. Aged only nine years Peter especially tugged at her and begged her not to go, but Alison pushed him away. I still cry when I think or write about it. Alison agreed to come with me to a counsellor but after two visits she would not change her mind and left our home to take a flat in the nearby suburb of Manly. I drove her to the flat hoping that way I would be able to keep in touch with her.

In fact one morning a day or two later I took our baby Katie to visit Alison hoping that seeing our baby might make her want to come home. She wasn't in but an attendant opened her door and allowed us to wait for her inside. I was further heartbroken when I noticed an ashtray beside the bed. There were several cigarette butts in the ashtray and only about half were stained by lipstick. Alison was still been denying that there was anyone else in her life and until that moment I had hoped the rumours were wrong. Katie and I went home without seeing her. I was confused. I still loved her yet I also hated her. I hated what she was doing and I hated anyone who was taking her away from us. My once dearly loved former Sunday-school teacher wife had taken up with someone else and I didn't know why. Even with all the years that have passed since I have still not understood. Alison has never explained why she left or what I had done wrong. At thirty-five she was surely too young to be having a 'mid-life crisis' but I had, and still have had, no other explanation than the example and persuasion of her so-called 'close friend'. For years I longed to see her but abused her when I did.

It came as no surprise to hear that her 'close friend' also left her husband, not to live with the schoolteacher, nor even with a young married man across the road with whom she was said to be involved, but with yet another man.

A couple of years earlier Alison's mother had died in Scotland and her elderly father had come out from Scotland to be close to us. Pop, as I called him, was very upset about Alison's behaviour and said he could not understand why. He offered to help in any way he could. For the next six months I would make the children their school lunch and breakfast and before packing them off for school I would pick up their grandpa who would then stay with Katie all day. I came home from the hospital every lunch-time to change and feed her and make sure Pop was all right, then go back to work and return in the evening to get the kiddies' dinner and take Pop home. I cried myself to sleep every night for weeks.

A special visiting Professorship

Before Alison left I had made one serious commitment for the following year that I felt obliged to keep. On Dr Dunphy's recommendation, supported by colleagues who remembered me in Portland and the Professor of Surgery whom I knew in Vancouver, Canada, I was invited to be the guest Professor at the special centenary meeting of the North-West Surgical Association, a very distinguished association of surgeons from the US states of Oregon and Washington and from British Columbia in Canada. The meeting was to consist of a week teaching and lecturing in each of Portland and Vancouver, and finally at the major meeting of the association in Seattle, Washington. Programs, invitations to special people and other arrangements had been made before Alison had left the family so I could not refuse. I arranged for a professional nanny to take care of the children. Meanwhile one of Alison's elderly aunts in England had heard of her departure and she took it upon herself to come to take care of the children while I was away.

Assured that there were two capable women caring for them I went off for three weeks and had happy and successful visits to Portland, Vancouver, and Seattle as well as a short visit to San Francisco. I regularly telephoned home and was told by one or other of the children's carers that all was well and not to worry.

At the end of the final meeting in Seattle I was thanked with a standing ovation and made an honorary fellow of their society. I was a little confused by the standing ovation but I later realised what a compliment it was. I flew home happy in the knowledge that my children had been well cared for – until I came in the front door where I was besieged by unhappy children who begged me not to go away again. Apparently the two women minders had disliked each other and the children had been caught up in unhappy turmoil.

I promised them I would not leave them again for any surgical meeting or anything else and with two exceptions, to which I was fully committed, I did not leave them in anyone else's care or accept overseas invitations for eight years. One of the exceptions was to give a paper on my work to the American College of Surgeons, as promised to Dr Dunphy a year previously. The other was to accept a commitment to be guest Professor in Melbourne University's medical school in Geelong in 1977. For these visits, I was away for only 12 days on each occasion and had a very reliable, experienced housekeeper/nanny whom all the children liked. Naturally with such domestic disruption my work was affected; my laboratory research came to a virtual halt but somehow I still managed to look after my patients and keep up my teaching.

In 1974 Alison served me with divorce papers so I consulted a solicitor who confirmed what I already knew in my heart but did not want to face. In her papers Alison admitted that she had a lover and wanted the law to consider this matter 'at its discretion'. She then learnt from her lawyer that large sums of alimony would not be awarded unless she took care of some of the children. She then offered to take two of the children and named the two she would be willing to have.

I refused her offer making it clear I would not allow the family to be broken up. If any court deprived me of any of the children I would insist Alison take them all rather than have the family more broken than it was. She then withdrew her application for divided custody, so they all stayed with me.

Single parent life with five children

Life as a sole parent to five children and a highly responsible busy job required my full attention. Cutting lunches, making dinners, shopping, washing clothes and dishes and trying to attend all school and sports functions was a very full occupation, especially as my oldest child Jenny was only 13 and Katie only one year old when their mother left home. However, I was determined that my children would live as normal a lifestyle as possible and that they would feel loved and each have the attention they needed. Nevertheless after Alison had been away for six months and Pop was becoming more fragile, I realised that I did need a 'live-in' housekeeper.

Interviewing applicants for the role of Stephens's family housekeeper was interesting. One or two expressed trepidation that I might expect them to be my bed-partner. I assured them that this was not the case, however, another was interested only on condition that sharing my bed would be part of the arrangement. She withdrew her application after I explained that this was not part of the deal. I did not want to complicate my housekeeping arrangements.

My first live-in housekeeper was Cindy, a pleasant young woman who took good care of my children. Unfortunately Cindy retired after the kids had made it clear that they did not want any woman other than their mother looking after them. None of my school-age children liked having housekeepers or any other women in the house. We went through a series of housekeepers, young, middle aged and older, but the kids managed to make things difficult for each of them, so after a while each of my housekeepers left.

The only long-term housekeeper that the children accepted was Estel, who was a pleasant and likeable young Spanish woman who had left her wife-beating husband and needed a job and a sanctuary for herself and her three year-old hyperactive son, Zac. We had Estel for about two years until she decided to take Zac back to Spain to permanently escape from her troublesome ex-husband. I took the opportunity of brushing up my Lillian-taught Spanish while Estel was with us and often wondered where Lillian was but did not know how to get in touch with her. Some years later Estel and Zac visited Australia and came to see us. Zac had grown into a tall, handsome young man, but could no longer speak English.

Live-in housekeepers were a great help but there are limits as to what a housekeeper can do, especially as the children resented housekeepers and each wanted their Dad's attention. Still, we did manage to celebrate all the birthdays, holidays and special events. At Christmas I always had a Christmas stocking for each of the children hanging on the railings of the staircase, but got into trouble one Christmas when I had had Christmas-eve dinner with my friends the McClures and arrived home rather late to find my younger children already out of bed and quite upset. They had risen a short time earlier to find that Santa Claus had not left them anything in their stockings. I had to explain that Santa had struck some bad weather at the North Pole and was running late.

The children always loved our annual visits to the Sydney Royal Easter Show and the Anzac Day march. Anzac Day was special to them because the march was along Macquarie Street past Sydney Hospital and we therefore always had good viewing positions. However, the Easter show was, for me, a test of endurance. Trying to keep four active children together when they were all interested in different things, while pushing Katie in a baby stroller, was quite demanding. We had mandatory inspections of the cows, horses and wood-chopping by Bobby; inspections of every individual pig by Peter (he always made a fuss if we missed one); and a look at every animal in the animal nursery for Jenny and Jill. Then we would stop for lunch and watch the ring events. After the annual disagreement among the kids as to when to stop watching the ring events, they would then eventually agree to look at the dogs, have the big slippery-dip rides, and make our way to the show-bag hall. There, with a limit of how much money each had to spend on show-bags it would take two or three circuits of the hall for final decisions to be made as to what show-bags represented best value for money. Finally, loaded with show-bags and partly eaten fairy-floss we would pack into the car and go home with much discussion about what they liked best, who bought the best show-bags and what they wanted to see again next year. It was always a day of fun, but each year I would arrive home exhausted, financially ruined, and resolving to think of a way of avoiding the Easter Show the following year.

Aside from the show and other regular family events there were also some occasions that I realised that I could be outmanoeuvred by even the youngest of my children. On one such occasion I took Katie, aged five, to a friend's place for lunch. My friend who had two children aged six and eight was very impressed when at the end of the meal Katie had eaten everything on her plate, because neither of her children was currently eating vegetables. I was impressed with Katie too, and told her how proud I was that she had even eaten the vegetables that I could never get her to eat at home. A few days later, however, I discovered just how she had managed to create such a good impression when I came to wash the jacket she had been wearing. The pockets were stuffed with pumpkin, potato, broccoli and peas. I suppose it might have been predictable that she has since become a successful lawyer. She understood even then the wisdom of not revealing everything you know unless absolutely necessary.

One last special visit to America

When Estel was with us I was able to accept my invitation to give a paper on my work at an American College of Surgeons meeting in SanFrancisco. I stayed with Dr and Mrs Dunphy and they tried to console me about my broken marriage by taking me to several functions in the company of Dr Dunphy's secretary, Joyce, who was also recently divorced.

Joyce was a lovely young woman about Alison's age whom I had always respected and liked. When I had worked in San Francisco she had always been helpful as chief administrative assistant to Dr Dunphy and my best source of advice about what was going on or who to see about hospital and university matters. Until I arrived in San Francisco I was unaware that she had split up with her husband so she and I consoled each other. We were happy together and developed a strong mutual bond that I think may have been love. I had never known Joyce's former husband but Joyce had known Alison fairly well. She told me that our separation may have been predictable because during our stay in San Francisco she and others had become aware that Alison appeared to have an interest in other men.

Joyce had no children and she and I talked about her coming to live with us in Australia but she was naturally very apprehensive about such a radical move. It would have meant leaving her job, her country and her family to share her life not only with me, but with my five children. I understood when she decided not to come and I was also aware that I could not compromise my primary responsibility of caring for my children by moving them from Australia – even though Dr Dunphy invited me to consider a very well endowed and appealing chair to develop surgical oncology in San Francisco. I realised how difficult it would be to take on the responsibility of becoming Head of a Department in a North American Medical School while attempting to settle my children into a new and different environment. I was therefore forced to decline the invitation and all it entailed.

Jenny goes to boarding school

At the age of fifteen Jenny developed behaviour problems and started associating with undesirable friends. Despite a change of school she continued to make friends with young social misfits who were having 'pot-smoking parties'. I disliked pot-smoking then and I still hate it in spite of protests from users that marijuana is a 'soft' drug and relatively harmless. I was convinced, and it is now well established, that marijuana has all the evils of cigarettes and alcohol and worse. Chronic pot-smoking carries a considerable risk to both reproductive and mental health. Eventually, in spite of protests from Alison to 'let her find herself', I sent Jenny to a country boarding school, New England Girls' School (NEGS) in Armidale, northern New South Wales. I explained to the headmistress why I wanted to send Jenny away from her present school and environment and she agreed to enrol her and do her best to help.

Fortunately Jenny did not carry out her threat to run away from school. I will always be grateful to the headmistress, Jan Milbourne, and the staff of NEGS because Jenny settled down there and learned to love the school. She also made good friends, one of whom has since been her bridesmaid and the godmother to her first child. She now thanks me for sending her to boarding school and says it was the best thing I could have done for her. She is now a schoolteacher herself, and a very devoted mother to three children. One aftermath of Jenny's experience was that I never had any similar problems or any overt misbehaviour from any of the other children. As teenagers I suspect that one or more of them probably did misbehave from time to time but not as overtly and defiantly as Jenny had. They did not want to be sent away to boarding school – especially to Armidale – one of the coldest places in New South Wales.

A new romance

Meanwhile I started socialising again. I dated young women whom I found attractive but I was reluctant to further complicate my life at home. Amongst my many different girlfriends I met an attractive woman at work, who for this book will remain nameless. She was divorced and had sole custody of her two children who were respectively one and three years older than Katie. After we dated for some time this new love interest came to live with me and to help care for my children, particularly Katie. All seemed to be well and we decided to marry but a year or so after our wedding I suddenly developed a serious health problem: I had a heart attack.

Heart trouble

In October 1979 I was performing a major, rather complicated operation for cancer on a man's throat and neck when I felt a sudden disturbance in my chest, irregular thumping of my heart, and some light-headedness. Fortunately I had no major pain but I knew I had had a heart attack. I felt rather 'light-headed'. Although I was being assisted by a very good young surgical registrar I knew I must call for a more experienced surgeon to continue with and complete the operation. I left the operating theatre leaving my patient under the care of the anaesthetist and my registrar for ten minutes or so but I could not find the help I needed. None of the senior surgeons was to be found so I just had to go back and finish the more difficult part of the operation and then leave my registrar to finish and close the wound.

I went straight from the operating theatre to my close friend Sol Posen, the hospital's Associate Professor of Medicine. Sol immediately arranged an electrocardiogram (ECG) that confirmed my self-diagnosis: I had had a coronary infarct. He arranged for me to be admitted under the care of our friend, Dr Gaston Bauer, who was then a specialist cardiologist at the Royal North Shore Hospital. Further tests were carried out including X-rays of the coronary arteries (coronary angiography). During this procedure I had a further episode of chest distress and was sent to the intensive care unit where I remained for 10 days. The X-rays confirmed that I had one complete blockage in a major coronary artery and a number of incomplete blockages in all three major arteries. Dr Bauer told me that I must have major coronary by-pass surgery, which was still in its infancy in 1979. Being a surgeon I did not like the thought of other people operating on me so I asked Gaston what the alternative was. 'The only alternative I know', he advised, 'would be to have a funeral.'

At that time the most experienced team in open-heart surgery in Australia was in St Vincent's Hospital under the care of a very distinguished heart surgeon, Dr Mark Shanahan, and his brilliant young assistant, Dr Victor Chang. Both Mark and Victor were my friends. They shared consulting rooms with each other and agreed that I needed fairly urgent coronary artery bypass surgery. Both had seen me professionally and when it came to making arrangements for my surgery they asked, 'Which one of us do you want to do the operation'. I explained that I wanted both of them there and to put in as many grafts as I would ever need because I would never want to come back for more. This they did and together they made six bypasses, which in 1979 was some sort of record. Veins were taken from both of my legs to provide enough graft material.

I thought my recovery was uneventful. It was, except that my wife asked when she might come to see me after the operation. The operation was to be at 1 o'clock on Wednesday afternoon (17 October 1979) and my wife was told to come at about 4 o'clock as I should be back in the recovery ward about then. Next thing I remembered was waking up and asking my wife for the time. She told me that it was 5 o'clock. I said: 'Well that didn't take long did it, I only went to the theatre at 1 o'clock'. She said, 'Yes, but that was on Wednesday, it is now 5 o'clock on Friday afternoon'.

Prior to my hospital admission I had been delighted and impressed at how remarkable the response of huge fungating breast cancers were to our continuous treatment with intra-arterial infusion chemotherapy, and what a great further response there had been from follow-up radiotherapy to the breast cancer region. In my hospital bed I took advantage of the opportunity to get on with writing one particular dramatic case report. (See Figures 4a, b and c in the Appendix). This was published in *The Lancet* in August 1980. Next day I was interviewed by a *Sydney Morning Herald* medical journalist and on 30 August I was surprised to see a report of this work published under front-page headlines in the *Sydney Morning Herald*.

Clinical consequences of heart surgery

After about 10 days in hospital I was allowed home with strict instructions and advice about what I should do to make a good recovery and maintain better health. I was not a smoker, and virtually a non-drinker, so the best advice included losing weight (I was a little overweight), exercising regularly and to stop worrying.

To stop worrying was unrealistic with five children to look after and a wife who was not relating well with my children. So in the absence of that possibility I was determined to lose weight. I kept to a strict Pritikin-type diet and exercised as much as possible. The diet consisted of eating plenty of fresh fruit and vegetables, avoiding processed food, especially white bread, white sugar and white rice or flour, and drinking skim milk only. I was to avoid sugar-filled drinks or sugared cereals, eat little or no meat, avoid animal fat, and regularly eat grilled or steamed fish (not fried or battered). I soon became accustomed to this diet and it worked. I lost so much weight that I had to have the waistlines of all of my trousers taken in. I exercised by taking longer and longer walks.

Further clinical consequences of heart surgery

One troubling, but temporary, consequence was that having had a heart attack when doing long and intricate major surgery made me a little apprehensive about performing such operations for fear of another cardiac episode. However, this apprehension soon left me and I again performed any surgery that my patients needed. But there were troubles brewing on the home front. My wife was being increasingly unpleasant to my children, especially by seeming to always blame little Katie whenever her own daughter did anything wrong. I had become fond of both of her children and was pleased to be their Dad but her daughter, who was a little attention-seeker, regularly strayed into fairly innocent mischief for which Katie inevitably took, or shared the blame. My older kids were able to cope for themselves but they were all worried about the treatment Katie was receiving: never physical hurt but constant scolding and emotional hurt. I knew this couldn't last so when my wife decided to leave and take up with her wealthy employer things at home became more settled. The children were happier but I was even busier and swore to myself that I would enjoy the company of girlfriends but would never marry again.

Exercise: the 'City to Surf'

As a refuge from the chaos of my everyday life I took to more and more exercise. Usually I walked to and from the Sydney Harbour ferry that took me to Circular Quay and walked the short distance from there to Sydney Hospital. My walk to and from the ferry was five kilometres each way. After becoming more fit I often walked across the Harbour Bridge to Sydney Hospital (eight kilometres each way). Then I took to running the famous 14 kilometre Sydney City-to-Surf race that is held every August. I ran 12 successive City-to-Surf races, most of them with a friend, former Qantas pilot Alan Somerville, who had been a patient and was always grateful that I had cured his large buttock cancer without the radical amputation that he had originally been advised to have. On two or three runs Jenny ran with me, on four or five little Katie ran with me, and eventually Sheilagh, a special lady who came into my life ran with me three or four times.

Dr Rowley Richards, who, like Weary Dunlop was a World War II hero, took a special role in caring for any health problems in people who ran the City-to-Surf. As an old friend he took a special interest in my running after coronary artery bypass surgery. He was always happy to confirm that I was in good shape at the end of each run.

Off and racing

Patients sometimes express their thanks and gratitude in unusual ways because I treated them without charge, as was then the custom in public hospitals. One very grateful old lady was concerned that I could not send her a bill. At the same time the Melanoma Unit was having a fundraising raffle for a share in a racehorse that had been given by a generous donor to raise research funds. My patient bought a ticket in the raffle and was bewildered when she won a share in a racehorse. As she lived in an inner city suburb and said she wasn't even sure which end of a racehorse started first she decided that I should have her share. I was overwhelmed and gratefully accepted her offer as I had always loved horses and was also interested in seeing them race. Thus I became a one-sixth owner in a racehorse named 'Brass Band'.

What fun it turned out to be. I joined the other five part-owners to form a syndicate to feed, house, train and race our 'Brass Band', a somewhat costly exercise but we had a lot of fun. 'Brass Band' was a very handsome chestnut and showed a lot of potential as a middle-distance runner. Each time the trainer said he was ready to win, our group would get excited and meet together at the races. We had a number of exciting days when our horse ran second or third but the only race he actually won was one that was supposed to have been 'just for a trial' in preparation for some later races. I think this was the only time the horse's trainer did not suggest we 'have a few dollars' on him. It was certainly the only time none of our syndicate was at the track. The race was the 'Mississippi Stakes' at Warwick Farm racecourse in Sydney on 27 July 1983.

Sheilagh – a special lady

In 1984 a special lady came into my life. In Sydney Hospital I was looking after a man who had terminal cancer. I had been asked to care for this man by my friends, the medical superintendent Dr John Watson, and his wife Rose. While this man was ill I became aware of a young woman who was regularly at his bedside giving comfort. Because the young woman seemed to be very close to him, I discussed the man's illness and inevitable death with her. I mentioned this to Rose and John Watson and I spoke of the extraordinary care and attention the young woman had given to my patient and what a lovely and attractive person she was. Rose told me her name and asked if I would like to meet her. I said 'yes' but what I did not know was that Rose had decided she would try to be a matchmaker. I accepted an invitation to a dinner party at the Watsons' home in Vaucluse. Little did either Sheilagh or I know that we were to be the only guests at Rose's dinner party.

We seemed to click immediately. Sheilagh was very attractive. Her pretty face covered in freckles and gentle personality appealed to me. It transpired that she had been a Dominican nun in a convent for 13 years before leaving the Order and coming to live in Sydney. Following the Watson's dinner party we made a date for dinner at the Tank Stream restaurant in Sydney. The Tank Stream is the little stream that provided fresh water for the original European settlement on the shore of Sydney Harbour. The stream has long since been built over but this one little restaurant in the basement of a city building was the last public place still available to sit beside it.

We enjoyed our dinner and agreed to meet again … and again … and again. When we were invited to the Watsons' home on another occasion I took my baby daughter Katie with me. (Katie was then 11 years old but she was still my baby.) All of my children were still suspicious of new women appearing in my life, but especially Katie.

On Sheilagh's fortieth birthday, when I first met most of her family, I also took Katie with me. Sheilagh was the fifth of nine children, eight daughters and one son, from Cowell, a fishing village in outback South Australia. I got on well with her mother, her brother and several of her sisters who were there. I subsequently took Sheilagh home to meet the rest of my children. From something of a suspicious beginning with my children the ice slowly melted – but it took a long time.

As always my first responsibility was to my children and so there was a great deal of adjusting to do on both sides, but Sheilagh's visits to our home gradually became more frequent and acceptable. Although Katie loved having a 'mother' interested in her it took some time before Sheilagh was really welcome. Sheilagh was especially concerned for Katie, who for a long time was suspicious of anyone else entering her father's life, but by that time the older children didn't express much emotion either way. Sheilagh wanted the children to accept her and she even took Katie with her for a holiday to visit her mother in Cowell, the fishing village where she had grown up and where her father, Michael Kelly, had been the town solicitor. Katie was made very welcome by Sheilagh's mother, Gabrielle, and enjoyed the holiday. I still cherish photographs of little Katie fishing in the waters of the harbour at Cowell with Sheilagh and her mother.

After they returned to Mosman Sheilagh sometimes stayed the night and eventually, two years after we first met, she formally moved into my home. Her presence meant that once again I was able to accept invitations to go interstate and overseas. At that time Jenny was living away from home but she got on well with Sheilagh. The older children who were still at home soon accepted that Sheilagh and I were sharing a deeper relationship but Katie continued to keep her distance for some years.

Sheilagh and I were hesitant to make our union official. My children and I had been hurt too much before. However, after 20 years together our union was absolutely stable and by then Sheilagh has long been totally accepted by our children so we began to talk seriously about legalising our relationship in a marriage ceremony.

When we finally did decide to have an official and ritual recognition of our relationship we did this with the good wishes of all my children and grandchildren in a lovely little St David's church in Kurrajong Heights near my childhood Kurmond home. Rose Watson was witness and our only guest (John was too ill to attend).

After living with Sheilagh for some years I received a letter from Lillian. In her letter Lillian told me that she had been married and had two sons. She still lived in Buenos Aires but she and her husband had been separated for some time. I showed this letter to Sheilagh who was very understanding. She agreed that I should write to Lillian and tell her the story of my life. Lillian and I have since been corresponding regularly, usually at Christmas and one or two times during the year. Sheilagh shares our letters and Lillian always includes Sheilagh in her greetings. I have been lucky that in different ways, over the years, I have enjoyed the love of these two very genteel ladies.

Chapter Seven

Life After Sydney Hospital

I had a serious setback in the re-establishment and acceptance of my work at the Royal Prince Alfred Hospital. After my heart surgery I was in general good health but some changes were needed in my blood-pressure medication. One night one of my former Sydney Hospital patients was admitted with an acute abdominal problem that needed emergency surgery. I began operating but during the operation I started to feel light headed just like the day that I had a heart attack when operating at Sydney Hospital three or four years previously. Realising that I might need someone to take over the operation before I had finished I called a friend who was an experienced surgeon on the hospital staff. He came immediately and finished the operation for me. It was just as well as I was feeling quite faint due, I am sure, to a sudden drop in my blood pressure. I subsequently had to have my blood-pressure medication changed. Although I had no further such problems during the next 12 years I think there were still staff members who thought I should give up major operative surgery.

Having been trained as a surgeon I enjoyed operative surgery, and I knew better than anyone else exactly what my patients needed. Whenever I needed to perform a complicated or prolonged surgical procedure after the above episode I tried to make sure that there was a skilled surgeon somewhere nearby in case I had another cardiac episode. Fortunately the episodes were never repeated and I did not require such help.

In most of our bone cancer patients my close friend in orthopaedic surgery, Dr Bill Marsden and I operated together, especially when resecting a cancer involving bone that required bone or joint reconstruction.

Regional chemotherapy to avoid limb amputation

In my latter years at Sydney Hospital and the early years at the Royal Prince Alfred Hospital I developed a close bond of cooperative management of patients with cancers in a limb with Dr Bill Marsden who was a brilliant orthopaedic surgeon. Bill, being most interested in cancers of the muscles and bones, had a number of patients referred to him with advanced cancers in a limb that traditionally would have required amputation. He asked me about trying to save these patients from amputation with my special technique in an attempt to make the cancers smaller and less aggressive so that they could be removed surgically without amputation.

Our first patient, a 17-year-old youth, was originally advised to have his right arm and shoulder amputated to treat a large bone cancer in his shoulder. With the cooperation of Dr Richard Fox, a young medical oncologist, I treated him using intra-arterial infusion of chemotherapy to the cancer. There was an impressive response. The cancer was very much reduced in size and Bill Marsden was able to remove the residual cancer remaining in bone. He reconstructed the shoulder and the young man did well. When last seen 10 years later he was not only well but he played tennis with his right arm.

Unfortunately for us Dr Fox accepted a position as Professor in Melbourne, but Bill and I had many similar good results with our combined treatment of many cancers in limbs. In fact we were able to avoid amputation in 80% of patients originally referred for amputation.

I was having similarly good results in treating other locally advanced cancers including some locally advanced breast cancers and head-and-neck cancers. Dr Richard Waugh, an excellent vascular radiologist at the Royal Prince Alfred Hospital, became interested in our work and devised techniques of placing small cannulas into arteries that supplied blood directly to a number of cancers, thus in some cases avoiding significant surgical operations that would otherwise have been needed to implant the cannulas precisely in the right position.

On one occasion, I believed that a cancer that had become attached to both the major artery and vein in a man's thigh before chemotherapy may need a grafted vascular reconstruction. I therefore arranged for my friend, Michael Stephen, a vascular surgeon specialist, to stand by. Michael had an interest in cancer as well as vascular surgery. I don't think he believed that the cancer would have responded so well that removing the artery and vein would not be required so he came to the operation anyhow. When we operated we were all impressed at how much the cancer had regressed. It was then simply removed without touching the artery or vein. (The change in this patient's cancer is shown in Figures 9c and 9d.)

With two exceptions medical oncologists at the Royal Prince Alfred Hospital saw no place for a surgical oncology unit. These exceptions were Professor Richard Fox and Associate Professor Michael Friedlander, but they were soon lost from the Royal Prince Alfred after accepting professorial appointments at the Royal Melbourne and the Prince of Wales Hospitals respectively. Others at the Royal Prince Alfred seemed to believe that it was not a surgeon's place to use chemotherapy – especially pre-operative 'induction' chemotherapy – and in particular that it should not be given by intra-arterial infusion. They knew that some, like Professor Loewenthal, had tried this without success and had often made serious mistakes.

I was also considered by some surgeons as something of an intruder who wanted to steal all cancer patients away from surgeons on the staff. To avoid upsetting surgeons who referred patients with non-resectable cancers I always adopted a policy of offering to refer the patients back to the referring surgeon for operation after their cancers had been reduced and made operable. By adopting this policy I would not reduce the surgeon's practice unless the surgeon wished me to perform the operation.

The Royal Australasian College of Surgeons

Frustrated by the situation, I sought a partial remedy by appealing to the surgical community generally, and met with Professor Bruce Gray who at that time was having similar frustrations in Perth, Western Australia, where he was having success in using integrated intra-arterial chemotherapy and surgery. We met with a small group of surgical colleagues who were interested in the overall care of cancer patients and we subsequently put a motion to the Royal Australasian College of Surgeons that the College should establish a specialist section of surgical oncology. There was an international precedent: a section of Surgical Oncology had by then been established in the American College of Surgeons. However, our proposal was rejected. The shadow of John Loewenthal, long since deceased, still influenced the Australasian College. Disappointed by the lack of interest in Australia, in contrast to strong recognition and support of such work overseas, especially in Europe, America, Israel and Japan, I thereafter lost interest in our Australasian College.

I am nevertheless pleased to say that the Royal Australasian College of Surgeons belatedly came into the 20th century shortly before that century ended by reversing its earlier decision. It then established a specialist section of Surgical Oncology. Unhappily this was too late for me, having passed retirement age I had by then ceased active clinical practice.

Years after I retired a very collaborative medical oncologist, Dr Michael Boyer, was appointed head of Medical Oncology at RPAH. I am sure that with the cooperation of Michael Boyer and several of his younger colleagues, Surgical Oncology can at last be developed as a special service at Sydney University. My immediate successor at Sydney University and the RPAH Surgical Oncology service, Professor John Thompson, is now in charge of the world's biggest and most successful Melanoma Unit (after the retirement of both Professor Milton and Professor McCarthy) and simply does not have the time, facilities, or space to further this work without the appointment of a new Professor and Professorial unit to support him.

Head of the Department of Surgery at the University of Sydney

In 1987 the head of the Sydney University Department of Surgery, Professor Tom Reeve, reached his retirement age and a new head had to be appointed. The senior Professor, Gerry Milton, declined to be nominated for the post and instead, in an act of loyalty and support, he nominated me. The department members agreed, particularly because they wanted someone in charge who would battle the administrators who were planning a reduction in the status and funding of the department.

At that time a new faculty Dean was to be elected. My colleague, Professor Jim Lawrence, Head of the Department of Medicine, and

I appreciated that the Professor of Physiology, John Young, was an enthusiastic and capable administrator, so we were pleased to support his nomination to the vacancy. I believed that John Young was a man of enthusiasm and integrity who would support progress in our department.

John Young began well as Dean by promoting a number of new initiatives and successfully concluding a number of others. With his support the university Senate also appointed me to a 'Personal Chair' of Surgery. This was a satisfying honour that I was very pleased to accept. I was grateful to Professor Young for his support and believed I might now have a real chance of establishing a unit in surgical oncology. However I soon became aware that increasing university-funding difficulties meant I had to give priority to maintaining the department's existing specialised units. Battles already needed to be fought against university funding authorities to retain all units in what was one of the world's most outstanding departments of surgery.

In his early months as Dean, John Young showed an unusual initiative and dedication to the needs of both the university and the Faculty of Medicine. A few months later I wrote to the Chancellor in support of John Young for the vacancy of the position of Vice-Chancellor, a position that had become vacant after the tragic death of our much loved Vice-Chancellor, John Ward, who had been killed in a train accident. John Young was not appointed to the position but he assumed more and more authority in his role as Dean.

Administrative and financial problems

Little more than a year after John Young's appointment as Dean he began to make it clear what his priorities would be. Being a basic scientist and not a clinician he increasingly wanted to reduce the clinical departments' share of faculty funding in favour of physiology, biochemistry, histology, and curriculum studies. Of the basic sciences he wanted to severely curtail the teaching of anatomy, and he also tried to reduce some of the teaching of pathology (the study of disease processes). I, and others, argued that knowledge of both human anatomy and pathology is fundamental to being a good doctor. The planned clinical teaching changes especially affected surgery but also medicine, obstetrics, gynaecology and psychiatry.

I argued constantly with John to try to prevent him reducing the funding of the Department of Surgery. Far from being able to establish a special unit in surgical oncology, I seemed to spend much of my time lobbying to save the Department of Surgery from piecemeal destruction.

The needs of surgery were not high on John Young's list of priorities. Quite the reverse; at various points during this period many of our excellent established specialised surgical units came under threat. John argued that such preclinical departments as physiology, biochemistry and histology had no outside means of financial support but that specialised clinical departments, and especially highly specialised surgical units such as the 'bionic ear' unit, should be able to fund themselves from clinical practice and teaching hospital support. He was not pleased when I insisted on defending each of the Department of Surgery's specialty units that were not only contributing to the care of deserving patients but were pioneering research and teaching in these important developing clinical fields.

He particularly wanted to remove the 'bionic ear' unit from the faculty budget, even though it was this unit that gave hearing to deaf children. John took the view that if such highly specialised units were to be developed in the university they could be justified only if they were able to support themselves financially. I refused to accept his reduction of the bionic ear program or any of our established units which were all high quality units, each offering the best care of patients and high quality research.

In these circumstances there was obviously no hope of further developing surgical oncology because John Young believed it would be an added burden to university and teaching hospital resources and finance. Much as I tried to convince him of the value of surgical oncology as a specialty surgical unit that should be supported, he refused to be persuaded but preferred to take advice of some who saw surgical oncology as infringing on their own territorial ambitions. He never attended any of my lectures nor did he accept my offer to present my work at one of his special Dean's 'lunchtime lectures'.

Another major impediment to setting up an independent unit was that my new commitments as Head of Department made it impossible for me to attend the Royal Prince Alfred Hospital head-and-neck cancer clinics. Prior to being appointed Head of the Department of Surgery I had started to have some success in persuading medical, radiotherapy and surgical colleagues in the head-and-neck cancer clinic that the old notion of failure of intra-arterial pre-operative chemotherapy should be re-examined. As department chairman I had other commitments on those clinic days, and without my being there, the clinics returned to the more traditional treatments.

Disappointingly too, I was asked to recommend someone for the newly created Chair of Orthopaedic Surgery in Brisbane. RPA had already lost its most interested medical oncologist, Professor Richard Fox, and now I felt I had to recommend Bill Marsden for the Brisbane post. Bill was certainly the best person to establish a Chair of Orthopaedic Surgery in Brisbane, but by recommending him for the position I lost my closest colleague in treating advanced limb cancers.

I had originally hoped that my new status would enable me to work closer with medical oncologists and on more equal terms to develop combined cancer treatments with them, but there were too many departmental responsibilities and I found I had no regular time to reliably devote to this plan. I always seemed to have a meeting to attend, and knowing there were increasing threats to the comprehensive integrity of the department I dared not to be at them. Our medical oncologists continued to work with the more traditional surgeons who were more readily available, and who were more prepared to accept a role of skilled operative technician rather than as a key planner of integrated treatments.

As time went by I developed another major concern about accepting the administrative role as departmental head: I was not really a skilled administrator, nor had I ever been very interested in finance or administration (my bank balance would attest to that). As well, I was becoming increasingly aware that my hearing was failing me during meetings. I often missed what was being said. On a couple of occasions I did consult an old ENT (ear, nose and throat) specialist friend but he persuaded me that I did not need hearing aids. He thought they would be more of a hindrance than help.

Without the skills of my secretary, Carmen Blake and those of the department's accounts officer, Bronwyn Fisher, administrative matters would have become somewhat disorganised.

After retiring I found that my difficulties with the Dean were not unique. My successors, Les Bokay (1993–1998), followed by John Harris (1998–2003) and then John Fletcher have all been very skilled surgical Professors and very worthy Heads of the Department of Surgery, but each faced difficulties in keeping all activities of this extraordinary multi-skilled university department from losing essential financial support.

'Selling' university titles

One of my repeated disagreements with the Dean was my opposition to his plan to award professorial titles to non-university surgeons and physicians. My department, and other clinical departments, expressed the opinion that the title of Professor was an honour that had to be earned by years of dedicated research, teaching and high quality, but largely unpaid, clinical work. I argued that the title 'Professor' should not be devalued, as had happened in America, by awarding it to people who had not earned it in the traditional way.

John Young assured me that he had only a very few worthy people in mind to be honoured by the award of a professorial title. They were people who had made exceptional contributions to the research and understanding of clinical and academic issues, and in some cases to the promotion of teaching and research in other countries, especially disadvantaged countries. He assured the faculty that these people would be exceptional and that each title would be reviewed every three years to ensure that their standard of teaching and research was being maintained. It would also be a requirement that people awarded such an honour would not use the title publicly without qualification of the word 'clinical'. There would be no conferring a title simply as a reward for teachers who forgo their teaching fees.

Based on these conditions the faculty approved, in principle, the elevation of a small number of 'clinical Professors' and 'clinical associate Professors'. John Young established an advisory committee, which was nominally independent, to recommend these few special appointments, but in true political form he did not appoint to his advisory committee anyone who would be likely to disagree with him about any controversial matters.

Before long almost anyone who would agree to take part in

medical school teaching programs without payment was awarded a university title. The awards were never reviewed and the recipients' agreed limitation of the use of these honorary titles was never policed. Other universities have followed suit, not only in their medical faculties, but also in other faculties and, like in America, the title of Professor as a title of distinction has been devalued so that it is now difficult to find an authoritative radio or television commentator who does not use the title 'Professor'. In America the title of 'Professor' was given to so many teachers in medicine and other professions that most medical graduates now prefer to use the title doctor regardless of any unique university academic ranking or distinction.

The special role of university academics has always been to practise and teach at a high standard, and to initiate research for better treatments and better understanding of the most difficult health problems. To achieve this, they usually limited private practice to their teaching hospitals rather than spending their time making large incomes elsewhere.

As Dean, having initiated the acceptance of often successful and wealthy private practitioners as clinical Professors, Professor Young needed to redress the financial imbalance by allowing university Professors to establish private practice in private clinics and hospitals not associated with their teaching hospitals. With increased incomes, clinical academics could thus financially support much of their research work. This allowed him to justify reductions to funding of clinical departments, but over time it has compromised both the total commitment of university academics to teaching and research in the university and its teaching hospitals, or in disadvantaged countries, and the allocation of faculty funds to support research.

Hearing troubles

Although my ENT friend had twice assured me that I did not have enough hearing loss to justify hearing aids my decreasing hearing was becoming a problem, especially at meetings of the department or Academic Board. I feel sure that I must have misheard critical discussions, but it wasn't until after one meeting in which I had thanked the Dean for his support of a particular motion – when in fact he had opposed it – that I knew for sure.

When near retirement I again consulted a hearing specialist, this time a younger man, Professor Bill Gibson who was head of our 'Bionic Ear' implant team. Bill told me my hearing was definitely a problem and he subsequently fitted me with hearing aids shortly before I went to a meeting in Paris. My conversational hearing was much better but I had to remove the hearing aids in the Paris traffic – the noise was almost unbearable. I have since learned that the hearing aids then available were a great help with one-to-one conversation but could be worse than useless if there was any background noise.

Between the devil and the deep blue sea

As head of department I was responsible for recommending appointments to departmental vacancies, including a number of professorships. I felt privileged to have such a role but on one occasion, the appointment of a Professor of surgery at The Royal North Shore Hospital, I was uncomfortable in making any recommendation at all, knowing the resentment that would result from the unsuccessful candidates and their supporters.

The outstanding group of applicants included several international applicants and three highly regarded candidates from our own department, one of whom was already a Professor in his own right. I would have preferred one of the three to be appointed, but unfortunately senior people at the Royal North Shore Hospital could not agree on their preferred applicant. Some even threatened to resign if either of the two local applicants was appointed ahead of their choice. John Young, the Dean, believed that all of the applicants were of high quality but wondered whether the Royal North Shore Hospital was becoming too incestuous in apparently insisting that the best applicant for any position would have to be someone from that hospital – but he would not hear of my suggestion that another very senior and successful Professor from another Sydney teaching hospital should be invited to accept the position in which he had privately expressed an interest to me.

No amount of conciliation could bring about a consensus, so the appointment's committee agreed to recommend an outstanding applicant from the UK, Dr Tony Watson, who had a distinguished record in the UK and was also an Honorary Professor in an

American University. Tony was an excellent choice, but I believe one of the lobby groups for a local applicant never forgave me for not insisting on the appointment of their favoured applicant. This was despite the fact that I insisted he be promoted from Senior Lecturer to Associate Professor along with the other unsuccessful hospital applicant who had been more favoured by the majority of clinical surgeons at the hospital.

Tony Watson was well accepted by the majority of both hospital and university people, but his authority was constantly undermined by the one bitterly disappointed Associate Professor. After four years of this treatment Tony's health suffered and he resigned. He returned to England where he was almost immediately appointed as a Professor of Surgery of London University in a London Teaching Hospital, the Royal Free Hospital. After this experience I felt some sympathy for John Loewenthal. It must have sometimes been impossible for him to please everybody in his decision-making.

Thus the position at the Royal North Shore Hospital was vacant again. I had by this stage retired and was not a member of the new appointments committee but I was asked my opinion. I agreed that the Associate Professor, whose mainly administrative supporters had been so resentful, should now be appointed. However I don't think this ever redeemed me in their eyes.

A decision to retire

Apart from my family, my work was my life, but in 1992, sixty-five was the expected retirement age. Much to the embarrassment of the university, equal opportunities people were challenging the retirement age rule. I made a pact with the Dean that I would retire in 1993 but on condition that he would recommend the appointment of a successor to a Chair of Surgical Oncology. To this he agreed but he broke this promise because, I believe, he was determined to take the opportunity of saving money by having one less Professor in the Department of Surgery.

Success in administration

I admired the enthusiasm of John Young for his work but in time did not admire his way of handling people and events. John Loewenthal and John Young aside, I always had happy and respectful relationships with our Faculty Deans (Frank McGary, Richard Gye and Stephen Leeder). I knew that whether or not I agreed with their decisions I was always given a fair hearing and could rely on their word as their bond. Some might say they were not as ambitious for themselves nor so determined to make faculty changes regardless of other opinions. With both John Loewenthal and John Young any semblance of democracy was 'guided'. Controversial matters were always referred to 'independent' advisory sub-committees, but the people appointed to such sub-committees were invariably people whose opinions were well known to the Dean or who had had personal discussions with him. I now realise that these are the methods of successful politicians, not just 'successful' university Deans. It is rather like appointing a sub-committee of three foxes and a duck to decide what they would eat for dinner.

I am now glad to have left the political 'bun-fighting' behind me. I recognise that I was not meant to be an administrator. I was too politically naïve, believing dedication and honesty would be enough.

Chapter Eight

A Worldwide Interest in Surgical Oncology

The beginning of many overseas invitations and visits

As a result of the papers published while I was recuperating from heart surgery I was invited as guest speaker (all expenses paid!) to Germany in 1982 to give the opening lecture at a conference on 'Regional Chemotherapy in Integrated Cancer Treatment'. It seemed there was increased interest in this work in many developed countries, except Australia. The first meeting attracted mostly surgeons, but also some physicians, haematologists, medical oncologists, radiotherapists, radiologists and pathologists from Germany, France, the US, Holland, Belgium, Yugoslavia, Italy, Denmark, Norway, Sweden, Israel, Japan and Taiwan – about 40 specialists in all.

Dr Karl Aigner in Giessen, Germany arranged the meeting. Dr 'Charlie' Aigner was then a senior lecturer in Professor Schwemlie's Department of Surgery in Giessen University in Germany. I had the wonderful experience of assisting Dr Aigner perform his second, and the world's second, operation in which a man's cancer-riddled liver was isolated from the rest of his body and perfused with blood with a high concentration of chemotherapy and then all successfully reconnected. Dr Aigner was truly a master of his operating surgical craft. I have seen and assisted many leading surgeons operate, but I have never before, or since, witnessed such technical dexterity and skill. The patient's cancer responded considerably but recurred about one year later.

Professor Aigner was my host on six occasions when he invited me to present my work at meetings in Germany.

After that initial meeting I was invited (again all expenses paid) to the Second International Conference on Anti-Cancer

Chemotherapy held in Paris. This was a big international meeting of predominantly of medical oncologists, held in the Palais des Congres, a multi-storey congress centre near the Arc de Triomphe. Professor Claude Jacqillat and Dr (now Professor) David Khayat were the Paris hosts, together with Professor Gabriel Hortobagi of America's largest cancer hospital, the MD Anderson Hospital, in Texas. All were distinguished medical oncologists, so I was quite flattered to have been invited and to be awarded the prize for the best international poster at the congress. My lecture and poster were about our work in Sydney using pre-operative intra-arterial chemotherapy as first treatment in an integrated treatment program for locally advanced cancers. Not only was I honoured to represent Australia at this congress, but subsequently I have been invited to all annual congresses that have been held in Paris since that year. I accepted all these invitations and gave papers at every congress until 1995, two years after my retirement from Sydney University. I still receive an invitation each year but, partly for health reasons, and partly due to the fact that I have retired and so have nothing new to offer in the field, I no longer accept the invitations to Paris.

In 1985 and every second year thereafter, the pioneering group that had first met in Giessen in 1982 reconvened in Germany. My younger son, Peter, came with me to the second meeting, also in Giessen. There were subsequently meetings held in Ulm (a wonderful Lutheran Cathedral city on the Danube), Trostberg (in Bavaria), Berchestgarten (in the beautiful Bavarian Alps where Adolf Hitler had his holiday hideaway), Rosenheim (also in Bavaria), and Wiesbaden (a German city near Frankfurt with old Roman hot spring baths). Meetings were held twice in each of Giessen, Wiesbaden and Ulm and by invitation I gave the opening paper at most of those them.

The International Society for Regional Cancer Therapy

At the 1989 meeting, held in the Bavarian city of Rosenheim, we decided that we would form an International Society for Regional Cancer Therapy. By then membership had grown to 200 regular attendees and I was proud to be elected the society's first president, a position I held for four years until my retirement from Sydney University and the Royal Prince Alfred Hospital.

In 1995 on my nomination Professor Aigner was elected president. Although retired from my university and hospital positions since 1993, I was invited to present my work, all expenses paid, at meetings in the US, Paris, Israel and Japan until 1999.

For the sake of convenience to everyone interested in new aspects of cancer therapy, the International Society for Regional Cancer Treatment meetings are now held annually in Paris in conjunction with the conferences on cancer. Also, the journal we started *Regional Cancer Treatment*, of which I was one of three managing editors, has now been incorporated into the *European Journal of Surgical Oncology* which was developed by a separate European surgical oncology group, the European Surgical Oncology Society. My younger Sydney University and Royal Prince Alfred colleague, Professor John Thompson, a brilliant surgeon and surgical oncologist, is now the Australian representative on both of these organisations. The Paris congresses now attract thousands of participants from all over the world.

Since Professor McCarthy retired, John Thompson also has the responsibility of being Head of Sydney's very busy Melanoma Unit. By virtue of a predominantly white, fair-skinned, out of doors-living and beach-loving society, Australia has the world's highest incidence of melanoma per head of population, so that the Sydney Melanoma Unit has become the biggest and busiest Melanoma Unit in the world. It is an almost impossible task to expect one Professor to continue the work of the Melanoma Unit and at the same time to continue development of our internationally regarded Surgical Oncology unit and its special work.

The invitations to speak overseas about our work in Sydney were the highlight of my career. Sheilagh came with me to some of the conferences but when she was not able to come due to her own work commitments I took either my son Peter, or one of my daughters Jill or Kate. My doctor son Bobby, who was doing postgraduate studies in dermatology in England, and his wife Rose, were also warmly welcomed to one of the meetings. My oldest daughter, Jenny, was fully occupied caring for her husband and three children, as well as being a full-time primary school teacher.

It was great to see the interest generated by our Sydney studies in important cancer centres in every western country – as well as in Japan, India, China and Taiwan. At home there had at last been acceptance of the value of pre-operative chemotherapy given systemically (intravenously) for some cancers, but there was still non-acceptance that pre-operative intra-arterial chemotherapy had anything special to offer. Most people were simply not prepared to be readily available day-and-night for up to five or six weeks. Shorter periods of intra-arterial infusion had been tried, but without as much success unless used in a 'closed circuit' circulation. This involved perfusing very concentrated doses of chemotherapy through a limb for an hour or so without circulating through the rest of the body.

I was so convinced of the potential for chemotherapy to be more effective with my technique that I arranged for a young medical researcher, Dr Gary Harker, to study this concept on a cancer that occurs naturally in Australian sheep. Sheep in Australia often develop a cancer in areas of the body that are not covered by wool, that is, the skin of face, nose and ears. This is a naturally occurring cancer, not an artificially induced cancer, or an implanted cancer, but a cancer that is caused by excessive sun exposure – just as it often occurs in people. Using this sheep model Dr Harker proved conclusively that the response in sheep cancers is much greater when chemotherapy is infused slowly over a period of about five weeks into the supplying artery directly rather than when the same doses are given intravenously over the same time period to the body as a whole. There were two exceptions to this finding. Two drugs need to circulate through the liver to become activated, hence there is no advantage in having them infused through the tumour first. This too was confirmed by Dr Harker's studies.

Dr Harker was meticulous – as human studies require – and was eventually awarded a PhD for his work. He was also awarded an international prize in Germany where researchers expressed envy that we had such a good cancer research model in Australian sun-exposed sheep.

In spite of this compelling evidence, and the fact that pre-operative intra-arterial infusion chemotherapy is being used in a number of oncology centres throughout the world (a Google literature search listed 412,000 published papers using intra-arterial infusion chemotherapy) it is, other than for treating secondary cancers in the liver, still rarely used in Australia. Admittedly, it is relatively expensive, sometimes requiring five or six weeks in a costly hospital bed under constant and close supervision by an experienced team of doctors and nurses. Also, randomised studies have not been conducted to convince statisticians of the value of the work – and that is a problem because cancer specialists, and especially some prominent medical oncologists in Sydney, were indoctrinated with the value of randomised statistical trials. They were unwilling to accept any other form of evidence to prove the truth of a study. The fact that the majority of patients treated by standard treatments did poorly, and the majority of similar patients treated by the new and different method did well, was not accepted as sufficient evidence.

Chapter Nine

Medical Politics, Regrets and Satisfied Patients

History of the administration of cancer organisations

In Sydney the first appointed medical oncologists battled with surgeons and radiotherapists (the traditional cancer specialists) for 'territorial rights' to decide overall patient management. Over time they gained control, not only of the Clinical Oncology Society of Australia (COSA), which I helped establish, but also of cancer appointment bodies and government cancer funding organisations. Some surgeons, who were happy to accept a role as operative surgical technicians, helped them. The attitude of some of those original medical oncologists has been that surgeons should 'cut up and shut up'. That is, in anything but straightforward cancer problems, surgeons should operate when the medical oncologists have decided that is the best course of action.

One of the major consequences of my lack of medico-political nous was that control of funds for cancer research lay predominantly with medical oncologists, so I had no alternative but to personally fund my own research work, which I did for years – although most of my travel expenses were paid by the overseas or interstate hosts.

It has been interesting to hear from colleagues in most European countries, the US, Canada, and Israel that the same early battle between surgeons and medical oncologists was initially a feature but gradually there developed mutual co-operation and harmony. I envied them because their experience was not replicated here. When I asked my friend from Japan, Professor Tetsuo Taguchi, whether he had any difficulty with gaining co-operation with medical oncologists I was amused by his answer: 'In Japan they do what I tell them to do'. Such was the authority of the senior surgical oncologist in Japan.

Some of the more thoughtful surgical pioneers of advanced cancer management techniques in Sydney still have difficulties with the present system. This was underlined by the resignation of one of Australia's outstanding professors of surgery, Professor David Morris of St George Hospital and the University of NSW, in protest at control of government funding by the now established astute medical political players. Since I retired a new generation of oncologists in Sydney have developed a more collaborative approach in deciding best courses of action for treatment of cancer patients in joint management clinics, but there is still no full-time designated professor of surgical oncology.

A lingering regret – still no properly funded Chair of Surgical Oncology in Sydney

Unhappily, due to continued lack of interest by major cancer lobby groups, neither the University of Sydney nor the Royal Prince Alfred Hospital has funded an independent chair of surgical oncology with facilities to continue the kind of clinical and research work in which we were once world leaders. To help redress the situation, funds are desperately needed for a new professorial chair in surgical oncology so that our leadership in surgical oncology might be re-established. Australia's outstanding work in the Sydney Melanoma Unit should not be compromised by retaining the present situation in which one Professor is expected to fill both research and clinical developments in both fields.

Several chairs of medical oncology are well established in Sydney University as well as its major teaching hospitals. They now play a major role in cancer care as well as research and teaching, but Sydney University also deserves a full chair of surgical oncology.

I have been disappointed that I was not able to persuade the powers that be that if they had developed Surgical Oncology, more of our patients could have been cured. Others may have avoided radical surgery, including limb amputation. I was not prepared to forsake patient care to become a more effective and virtually full-time lobbyist. Being prepared to tell stories, write reports and massage the egos of gullible politicians and administrative heads is still the most effective method of advocating a cause in medico-politics, and in the long run it does get things done. The all too obvious

'I will scratch your back and say what a jolly good fellow you are if you will appoint me to a well-paid powerful administrative position' is not for me, nor has it been readily accepted by some of my most skilled colleagues, who are brilliant clinicians but are not skilled administrators and remain politically side-lined.

Political manipulation or skilled administration?

Despite my reservations about the ethics of some of their administrative methods, I readily acknowledge that John Loewenthal was largely responsible for building one of the world's best and most comprehensive departments of surgery and John Young developed perhaps Australia's most highly regarded medical school through introducing initiatives that selected most appropriate medical students for an innovative new medical school curriculum.

It still amazes me that Professor Loewenthal was given the necessary authority to build Westmead Hospital unencumbered by the opinions of any possible rival. It was obvious that a senior physician had to be involved in planning Westmead, but somehow he managed to appoint the junior of the two professors of medicine, the late Professor John Read, rather than the head of the department of medicine and most eminent professor, Professor Ruthven Blackburn, who may have preferred some things done differently. All this in spite of the opposition of both Professor Loewenthal and Professor Read to the concept of a teaching hospital so far from the university when that offer was first made to the directors of Sydney Hospital. I have since learned that those who are best at playing politics will always come out on top.

True satisfaction

I have been lucky to have made many good friends throughout my life. I still keep in touch with many of my old friends from Kurmond, my high schools, my church youth club the OKs (Order of Knights), my days as a trainee resident doctor in Australia, England and Scotland, my ship's surgeon days, as well as my later years. I have also been fortunate in maintaining friendships with colleagues in many countries that I have visited during my career, especially in the USA, England, Scotland, Wales, Ireland, Germany, France, Holland, the US, Canada, New Zealand, Israel, Japan and Taiwan.

Thanks from patients more than 20 years after treatment

One special bond that gives me great satisfaction and real pleasure is that I still receive cards, letters, telephone calls and even presents from many former patients who I am privileged to now count as friends. These are former patients who remain alive and well many years after having been told that they had a virtually incurable cancer, or at least a cancer that would have required amputation or extensive radical surgery with tissue reconstruction to have any hope of cure. Most of these are not people who had widespread cancer but very advanced, previously untreated local cancers, including cancers in the mouth and throat, breast, stomach, liver and limbs; they are people who had been advised by their doctors that a cure was either not possible or at least not possible without very radical or mutilating surgery.

Some former patients, who are well more than 20 years after treatment and still keep in touch with me, include the former World War II airman and Qantas pilot, **Alan Somerville** of Clontarf, whom I mentioned earlier. With our integrated treatment Alan's leg and buttock were saved and he became a keen runner after his treatment and ran 12 city-to-surf races, most of them with me. Well into his eighties he regularly ran shorter distances. Sadly Alan died of unrelated causes at the age of 87 in April 2008.

Another 20 years plus survivor is **Pat Fordham** of Menangle, a former nurse, referred to me by a surgical colleague when he found many small metastatic cancers in her liver after resection of a bowel cancer. After implanting a continuous infusion pump to deliver chemotherapy directly into the artery supplying blood to her liver, Pat returned to nursing for about twelve years (she has since retired) and still has no evidence of cancer.

Other members of this patient-cum-friend group, who have survived more than twenty post-treatment years are; **Mercedes Nardella** of Kingsgrove who avoided radical surgery to her palate in 1976, and **Neta Salter** of Cundletown who was referred by a distinguished surgical colleague in 1977 in the hope of avoiding an attempt at curing her advanced lower lip cancer that would have required total removal of the lower lip with plastic reconstruction of a new lip. Her cancer responded well to our integrated treatment leaving only a small residual cancer that was simply excised and repaired. Both Mercedes and Neta were well when we last spoke on the telephone in 2007.

Ian Kierce of Banora Point was referred to me in 1978 with several cancers in his mouth and tongue. His cancers responded well to continuous intra-arterial infusion chemotherapy and totally disappeared after follow-up radiotherapy. He has not needed surgery. He has had no mouth cancer and spoke well when we last made telephone contact (2007).

Lorna Ticehurst of Guildford was referred with an advanced cancer in her mouth that had spread into lymph nodes in her neck. She responded well to continuous intra-arterial chemotherapy for four weeks followed by surgery and more than 20 years later (2007) she spoke well to me on the telephone and assured me that she has had no further cancer trouble.

Margaret Hayden of Dundas, a medical colleague's wife, avoided radical surgery in her mouth and cheek in 1980, and remains well. Margaret never fails to send me a Christmas card every year since her treatment.

Peter Schwenke of Glenfield was referred by a highly skilled surgeon in 1981 for treatment of an 'inoperable' cancer of the floor of his mouth and tongue. After combined, integrated treatment Peter is well. He was free of cancer when we last spoke in 2007 and he keeps in regular touch by email.

I also hear regularly from **Patrick Kennedy** of Davidson, a former neighbour, who in 1984 rejected the advice of a leading head and neck surgeon that he should have radical surgery for his extensive throat and palate cancer, which in those days had about a 20% chance of cure by surgery alone or even by surgery and radiotherapy. He remains well after being treated by continuous intra-arterial chemotherapy followed three weeks later by radiotherapy.

Andrew Mitchell of Waverly was referred to me by an eminent surgeon who had not been able to totally remove a cancer in the parotid gland. After our treatment Andrew remained well and cancer free for more than 20 years but unfortunately he recently advised me that he had developed a different cancer in his mouth.

Basil Kaplan of Vaucluse remains well and walks comfortably with two legs since he avoided above knee amputation for a large malignant tumour in his lower thigh in 1984 (see clinical illustrations).

Jessie Ritchie of Leichhardt also keeps in touch regularly. In 1985, Jessie had a large fixed, cancer in her groin for which she had refused a hind-quarter (lower limb and buttock) amputation that had been recommended by an eminent surgeon. This was avoided and Jessie still has two legs and walks well.

At the age of fifteen, **Peta Hinton** of Penshurst was referred with a bone cancer in her lower thigh (osteogenic sarcoma). Rather than amputation she elected to be treated by intra-arterial chemotherapy, excision of the diseased section of bone, and bone reconstruction (by Professor Marsden). She is now a respected artist and will be 35 this year. She walks well and has been free of cancer since her treatment.

Giustina Nigro was fourteen when she had a similar bone cancer treated in a similar way. She now lives in Perth. Dr Paul Stalley, Professor Marsden's successor, recently heard from her that she remains well and cancer free but she has needed some adjustment to her prosthesis.

Kylie Hoogerdyk of Barrack Heights was twenty-one when in 1988 she presented with a similar bone cancer of her lower left femur. She was given similar treatment with intra-arterial chemotherapy followed by excision of her lower femur replaced by a prosthesis (by Professor Marsden). She now has a beautiful baby girl and still occasionally sees Dr Stalley for adjustment of her prosthesis.

In 1983 **Arthur McGuiness** of Wentworthville was first referred to me for treatment of a large stomach cancer. We kept in touch until he died 20 years later from other causes not related to his stomach cancer.

In 1983 Professor Bill McCarthy referred **Catherine Harrison,** aged 48 of Coonamble, to me. Mrs Harrison had a huge neglected cancer involving most of her left breast and overlying skin. It was considered unlikely to be totally removable by surgery alone. The cancer was treated with a course of five weeks continuous intra-arterial chemotherapy to which it responded well. After it had been much reduced in size the region was given a course of radiotherapy by Dr Hambly. The residual breast was then totally excised and the resulting defect was closed with a full thickness (skin and fat) rotation flap from over her back muscles (see Figure 7). Mrs Harrison was well and cancer free when we last spoke by telephone in 2010.

A remarkable patient whom I first treated in 1977 was **Philip Worsley** of Newport, NSW. Philip was referred to me by a highly regarded surgeon because he had operated in an attempt to remove a grapefruit sized painful primary cancer in his liver (such cancers are rare in Australia). At operation after examining the cancer the surgeon decided that it could not be resected, not only because of its position and size, but it was adherent to the major abdominal vein under the liver (the vena cava); so he was referred to our Sydney Hospital unit in the hope that we could do something to help and especially to relieve his pain. After treatment with continuous intra-arterial chemotherapy for five weeks the lump was much reduced in size and the pain was much relieved. Knowing of the difficulties of resecting such a lesion, even though it had been greatly reduced in size, the surgeon concerned and I agreed to send Philip to Hong Kong for the world's most experienced surgeon in liver cancers, Professor G.B. Ong, to resect if possible. Professor Ong and his then assistant (now Professor) John Wong successfully resected the cancer. When I last spoke with Philip (2007) other than being troubled with diabetes he was well but I was sorry to learn that he died of a disease unrelated to cancer in 2009.

After deciding in 1985 that I should once more try to develop a collegial working relationship with the Medical Oncology unit at the Royal Prince Alfred Hospital, I asked for a joint consultation with one of the medical oncology team about two women, **Bev Melton** of Cowra and **Diana Rosenbaum** of Gloucester, who had advanced breast cancers which they had been told were incurable. I told the medical oncologist of my plan to try to reduce these cancers with intra-arterial chemotherapy as a first stage of integrated treatment. When his registrar spoke to these women he told them both that there was no possibility of cure and that they should prepare for 'the inevitable', meaning their death within 12 months. Both women were terrified and asked me not to let 'that man' see them again. After our integrated treatment program both of these women are well. I still receive Christmas cards from each of them after 24 years.

Most of these long-term patients who still keep in touch were treated when I was at Sydney Hospital. That was when I had close cooperation and support from Fred Gunz and Colin Hambly, as well as the young, up-and-coming, pathologist, Stan McCarthy but some were treated soon after I first moved to the Royal Prince Alfred Hospital. Although my patients came from widespread parts of Australia and the Pacific Islands most of the people who still keep in touch live in Sydney or regional New South Wales.

At Sydney Hospital I had no trouble having patients stay as 'in-patients' for up to five or six weeks because the success rate was keenly noted by Doctors Gunz, Hambly, successive medical superintendents, and Professor Milton, who also began referring patients to me. Each medical superintendent knew that I was one of the original promoters of 'Outpatient' or 'Day Stay' surgery, and that I did not keep any patient in hospital longer than necessary. One of the many wonderful features of Sydney Hospital was that it was small enough for the medical superintendent to keep in touch with and show a keen interest in developments personally.

With too many sceptics, competing interests, and without the same team atmosphere at the Royal Prince Alfred Hospital, my work never regained its momentum after the enforced move from Sydney Hospital. Nevertheless, with the co-operation of pathologist Stan McCarthy (now transferred from Sydney to the Royal Prince Alfred Hospital) and Bill Marsden, and initially medical oncologist Richard Fox, and staff radiologist Dr Richard Waugh, our limb amputation prevention work (now called 'limb salvage') was continued.

Increasingly at the time, and more certainly nowadays, the limiting factor in arranging pre-operative intra-arterial chemotherapy for locally advanced cancers is that most of these patients require constant observation and care in hospital for up to six weeks. In present-day hospital economics it is difficult to arrange five or six weeks' continuous hospital care, even for patients with very advanced cancers. Hospital bed stays are increasingly expensive.

However, the irony of my life's work, depending so heavily on the economics of hospital admissions, was that my earlier work in Scotland helped pioneer the saving of millions of health dollars in Australia and hundreds of millions the world over through the reduced hospital stays of adult patients scheduled for 'outpatient' or 'day surgery' under a general anaesthetic. The feasibility, practicality and safety of performing this bed-saving and cost-saving surgery was established by Professor Dudley and myself in 1961 when we published our first two years' experience in Scotland in *The Lancet*.

Chapter 10

Frustration and Fulfilment in Retirement

Having been busy in active clinical practice virtually all of my working life, I found it difficult to contemplate retiring into nothingness, or even worse, filling in time by playing golf, sailing, or fishing. Knowing that the Melanoma Unit continued to be very busy, I arranged with Professor McCarthy to help in the Melanoma Unit clinics where I could also see some of my previously treated cancer patients who did not wish to transfer to another specialist doctor.

The author

I also had time to complete an ambition I had harboured for many years but left unfulfilled because of heavy clinical, teaching, research, administrative and family duties. I began writing books to help cancer patients understand their condition.

So often in my own practice patients would say a doctor had told them that they had a cancer, but apart from being terrified, they did not really know what a cancer was or how they might be affected. Even if their doctor had explained everything the stress of hearing the diagnosis meant they often could not understand or remember what was said.

Before I 'retired' I made several false starts to write a book that would explain cancer in language that my patients could easily understand. I wanted them to be able to read about it in the comfort of their own homes with family, friends or other loved ones around them. At least then they would be able to discuss it properly with their doctor on their next visit. But it wasn't until I did eventually retire that I really got into writing.

I called my first book *Cancer Explained*. Wakefield Press published it in 1997. The manager of Wakefield Press, Michael Bollen, is a genuinely compassionate and community-minded man. He was pleased to publish the book, which he realised was much needed by cancer patients. It was a pleasure to see this book being heavily promoted by the *Medical Journal of Australia* and by my radio medical broadcasting friends, Dr James Wright and Mr Alan Jones. I was flattered when the Managing Director of Gill and Macmillan, a publishing company in Ireland, asked for permission to publish an edition of the book the same year, with the agreement of Wakefield Press.

After publication of *Cancer Explained*, Rupert Murdoch's News Ltd asked me to write a booklet for incorporation in all its Australian daily and/or Sunday newspapers. The booklet, titled *Cancer an Explanation and Prevention* was circulated in all the company's daily and Sunday newspapers in every Australian State and Territory. Two other Australian companies, the Sanitarium Food Company and Santos Oil and Gas Ltd, also distributed it to all their respective workforces.

As *Cancer Explained* was first published in 1997 and many advances have subsequently been made in cancer understanding and cancer management, my friend and medical oncology colleague in Melbourne, Professor Richard Fox, joined me in writing a new updated edition of the book which was published by Random House in 2008. This book is also to be published in Braille and Large Print editions.

I was also approached by a number of men who were concerned about prostate cancer. Having heard so many conflicting recommendations about the most appropriate methods of detection and treatment they suggested that I should write a book about prostate cancer and its controversies, in everyday language people could understand. The result was the second book in this series *All About Prostate Cancer*. Some people wrote to me from overseas so I approached Oxford University Press about publishing the book. Oxford Press agreed and published *All About Prostate Cancer* in Melbourne in 2000. I am pleased to report that it had an excellent review in *The Lancet*, the world's leading medical journal, and a second printing was required in 2002. *The Lancet* reviewer summed up thus: 'I wholeheartedly recommend this book – these are things all men need to know'.

In addition, several women who were worried about breast cancer asked me to write a book on breast cancer that they could easily understand. Again Oxford University Press published *All About Breast Cancer* in 2001. It too had an excellent review in *The Lancet*: 'This combination of content and style puts *All About Breast Cancer* in a class of its own among consumer-orientated medical texts'.

Eventually my daughter Jenny, who had three young kiddies, asked me to write a book on cancer prevention. This made a lot of sense to me so I wrote *The Cancer Prevention Manual.* This time Oxford University Press asked me to agree to have the book published in the UK where it was nominated for a 'best book prize' of the British Medical Association. I believe *The Cancer Prevention Manual* is the most important book I have written. It is imperative for young people and carers of children to develop good habits early in life. With good habits the risk of getting cancer later in life is greatly diminished. I have given a copy of these books to several schools that I or my children or grandchildren have been associated with, but I don't have the resources to present a book to every home or every school, which is what I would like to do.

Inevitable prejudice

Although all of my books have been highly recommended in Britain and/or Ireland and have sold well in other countries, it is disappointing to know that none of them appears on the Australian Cancer Society's list of recommended reading for lay readers. *The Cancer Prevention Manual* is not even on the Australian Cancer Council's recommended reading list, even though it was so highly rated by Oxford University Press. Such is the defensive nature of some of the people who have been appointed to government cancer bodies in Australia, that because the books were not written by one of them or one of their close associates, the books have not received due recognition.

I have sent one or other of my books to notable people and organisations and, with some significant exceptions, every politician, university or health administrator, leading medical and nonmedical broadcaster, school headmaster and leading sportsperson to whom I have sent a copy has written a letter of thanks. For example I received acknowledgements from John Howard, the former Prime Minister; the Governor of New South Wales; Mr Tony Abbott (as the former Federal Minister for Health); the Vice Chancellor and Principal of the University of Sydney; several overseas Professors of Surgical and Medical Oncology and Directors of Cancer Clinics, the late Jane McGrath, much admired wife of former great cricketer, Glen McGrath – and even the late Sir Donald Bradman, my sporting hero, whom I first saw with my Dad playing cricket on the Sydney Cricket Ground more than 60 years previously.

Each of these very busy people found time to acknowledge and comment on my books – but I have not even had any acknowledgement of receiving the books from government officials most intimately involved with administration of cancer services. This administrative 'in group' apparently decided that it alone should control the dissemination of all cancer information as well as services. Consequently they have ignored my books, despite the books' endorsement by highly reputable international bodies.

I believe that this dismissal of my books is related to the longstanding rivalries between me, as a surgical oncologist, and the non-surgical cancer administrative establishment that I referred to earlier in this book. Although long-lasting in Australia similar rivalries have in the past been part of the development of cancer services in most developed countries where surgeons were expected to play little more than a technical operative role in cancer care.

Administrators

To paraphrase Winston Churchill: 'I always hope to have an executive who knows what should be done and does it. If not available I choose to have an executive who knows what should be done but does not get it done. If not available I would choose to have an executive who does not know what is needed but does not do anything anyhow. But God save me from an executive who does not know what is needed but does things regardless!'

I recognise the importance and value of good administrators but I have enough personal insight to know that I am not a good administrator. Administration and all the meetings, dealings, compromises, grooming contacts and such have never interested me. Although I did not always appreciate the personal styles of Professor John Loewenthal and Professor John Young, they did have notable successes in medical administration. Unfortunately they also ensured that administration of cancer services in New South Wales would remain for years in the hands of people who have not supported surgical oncology as an independent discipline.

By the time I began to write this story in 2006 I realised that there was a generation of younger medical oncologists with well-established units with whom I could have worked very well. Unfortunately, having now retired it is all too late for me. However, if a Department of Surgical Oncology were now to be established I am sure that these younger men and women would co-operate with a professor and his or her team in the establishment of a much needed comprehensive cancer centre.

More books

In June 2009 the major international textbook publisher, Springer Press, published my major textbook for students, medical practitioners, oncology nurses and medical scientists: *Basics of Oncology.* My co-author was Professor Karl Aigner of Germany, supported by contributing international cancer experts who are Professors of Medical or Surgical Oncology at leading cancer centres in England, America, France, Japan and Australia. This book is already in its second printing and at the request of some Spanish speaking doctors it is to be published in Spanish.

Springer Press has now contracted Professor Aigner and me to write a book on the specialist area of greatest interest to us to be called *Induction Chemotherapy – Integrated treatment programs for regionally advanced and aggressive cancers.*

For light relief I am also writing a book titled, *Laughter is Good Medicine.* For many years, beginning with my ship's surgeon days, I have written funny anecdotes, stories, incidents, jokes and other amusing stories or reflections in the back of my diaries. There is no 'dirt for dirt's sake', but there are some jokes or stories that I would not tell my mother or a clergyman of my own faith. I think this politically incorrect collection probably contains something to tease every race, sex, age group, religion, and nationality – except perhaps the Irish. Irish people seem to be the most prolific tellers of Irish jokes, which is why it isn't easy to find something funny to offend them. The exception to this Irish rule is Sheilagh, my wife. Although Sheilagh insists that the reason she rarely laughs at my jokes is not that she is offended, but simply that she is mystified by how she could have married a man with such a warped sense of humour.

Further health problems

Apart from issues resulting from my cardiac problems and my broken leg, a number of other health troubles caught up with me.

After a routine prostate (PSA) test was found to be raised in 1995 and further raised three months later, biopsies confirmed that I had early prostate cancer. Being a surgeon and in good general health I consulted a friend and leading Sydney urologist, Dr John Rogers. I agreed with his advice to have my prostate surgically removed. I am glad to say now, more than twelve years later, that I remain well. Prostatectomy is not always the most appropriate treatment for prostate cancer but obviously there is more about why I made that choice personally in my book *All About Prostate Cancer*.

Following the example of such pioneers as Edward Jenner, who used himself as an experimental model that vaccination with chicken-pox virus would prevent small-pox I decided to test on myself my belief that one reason to explain why prostate cancer is uncommon in people living in East-Asian countries is because they eat high soy diets which are high in plant hormones (phytoestrogens). Such plant hormones seem to be protective against certain cancers, including prostate cancer and breast cancer. I took by mouth relatively high doses of phytoestrogens each day for two weeks before having my prostate removed and arranged for my initial biopsy, which showed a moderately aggressive prostate cancer, to be compared with the cancer cells in my prostate after prostatectomy and therefore after two weeks of extra phytoestrogens in my diet. Much as I regretted having my prostate removed it was interesting to learn that the cancer cells remaining in the prostate appeared significantly less aggressive. This finding was published in the *Medical Journal of Australia* in 1997.

In 2001 I was having episodes of light-headedness associated with heart irregularities, a condition called 'intermittent auricular fibrillation'. On three occasions I had a 'blackout'. My cardiologist, Dr Kevin Hellestrand, who, many years previously, had been my registrar in Sydney Hospital and is now a close friend, told me that I had to have an immediate operation to implant a pacemaker. He insisted that I must have it 'tomorrow'. When I asked why it was so urgent he replied, 'Because you are driving on the same roads as I drive on and I don't want you blacking out and running into me'.

I duly had a pacemaker implanted and have had no such cardiac trouble since. By then it was 23 years since I had had six coronary artery bypass grafts. It is now more than 31 years.

Later in 2001 I was beginning to have eye problems due to cataracts in one eye and then the other. I first became aware of the cataracts during the performance of minor surgery when I realised that my vision was not as acute as it used to be. A surgeon who performs even minor operations needs to have excellent vision. I consulted a highly regarded Sydney Hospital colleague, Dr Alex Hunyer, who performed a cataract operation on each of my eyes at different times with excellent results.

A distinct advantage of knowing the very top members of the medical profession is that I have always known whom to consult and care for my various health problems and those of my family and friends. Over the years I am often asked by doctors, as well as my family and friends, who best to consult about a cancer problem or some other health matter. I have always been happy to advise or to suggest people to ask for such advice. When I retired I suggested to the Cancer Council and to state health authorities that a non-profit advisory panel should be established to help doctors, and especially country doctors, in their decision-making about where to seek the most expert help for their patients with difficult cancer or other health problems. I suggested that retired specialists with no personal or financial interest in advice given should staff such a panel, on a voluntary basis. I would be pleased to be an unpaid member of such an advisory panel. My suggestion was not implemented but I am still asked for such advice almost daily.

After these several health problems and despite continuing to enjoy seeing and helping patients I decided to call it a day and retire from all clinical work when I turned seventy-five in 2002. I planned to spend more time writing books, enjoying the company of my family, my grandchildren and friends – and especially Sheilagh with whom I wanted to visit those parts of Australia that neither of us had ever seen.

A broken promise

In 1998 I was asked by a very wealthy widow to visit the Philippines where her mother lived and had been diagnosed as having cancer of the pancreas. She hoped that I could do something to help her 80-year-old mother. Having read one of my books the woman expressed an interest in our work in Sydney and asked what fee I would charge to go to the Philippines to consult with her mother's medical team. I told her that I would come out of my clinical retirement to see if I could help but would not charge a fee because she offered to use her wealth and influence to help establish a Chair of Surgical Oncology at the University of Sydney. I was encouraged by this and persuaded my younger colleague, Professor John Thompson, to accompany me.

When we saw the lady's mother we advised that her doctors should not subject this elderly lady to the second major operation they had planned. We believed that she would be unlikely to survive any further major surgery. We also believed that her present symptoms were related to a dietary indiscretion in eating 'a feed of prawns' very soon after her major surgery only a week or so previously. In fact we did not see any convincing evidence that she had a cancer of the pancreas in the first place. It seemed to us that she probably had suffered from another pancreatic problem. We advised that no further surgery should be done. We understand that the old lady was soon discharged from hospital feeling relatively well and that she lived peacefully and comfortably for about another year.

Unfortunately no financial or any other help came from our wealthy widow 'friend', not even a 'thank you' letter and needless to say, the Chair of Surgical Oncology has never materialised.

Proposals for a comprehensive Cancer Centre to be established in Sydney without a specialist Department of Surgical Oncology

In recent years there have been proposals to establish a comprehensive Cancer Centre that would provide specialist management of patients with difficult or advanced cancers, initiate research programs, and offer management advice to medical practitioners.

Management of difficult cancers has progressed considerably since the days when treatment was primarily in the hands of either a surgeon, a radiotherapist or a chemotherapist. A comprehensive management team requires not just a surgeon but a surgical oncologist familiar with all surgical management and also practised in the different timing and methods of delivery of anti-cancer drugs in relation to surgery. It requires not only a radiotherapist but also a radiation oncologist skilled and practised in different types of radiation, radiation schedules and their doses and timing in relation to delivery of anti-cancer drugs. It also requires not just a chemotherapist but a medical oncologist familiar with the most effective drug schedules for different cancers and timing of their delivery to ensure the best protection against undesirable side-effects. Each of these experts should be familiar with what the other medicos in the team have to offer.

Australia is fortunate to have specialists in medical oncology and radiation oncology, some of whom have academic appointments that ensure total dedication to their specialty. Unfortunately, there is still no equivalent full-time chair in surgical oncology. This continues to be a deficiency in establishing a fully comprehensive Cancer Centre.

A comprehensive cancer centre can no longer be considered complete without a broadly experienced Department of Surgical Oncology. Hopefully such a department will be established in The University of Sydney, even though it is about 30 years late.

Unexpected tributes

Although riches, power, honour and glory have never been important to me other than as a means of providing well for my family, and for securing the best facilities for care of my patients, I confess that like everyone else it has been a great comfort to know that my work has been appreciated. Over the years, as a result, I have received a number of awards. These have included the Queen's Jubilee Medal, Membership of the Order of Australia (AM), Life Member of Sydney University Faculty of Medicine, citations in *Who's Who in Australia, Who's Who in America, Who's Who in Medicine, Who's Who in Science and Engineering* and *Who's Who in the World*, the Cambridge Biographical Centre publication *2000 Outstanding Intellectuals of the 21st Century* and a nomination for Australian of the Year. I would like to thank all of those who put my name forward for these honours. It is deeply satisfying to have one's efforts so well appreciated.

Another unexpected honour came from one of my former surgical registrars, Dr Chris Hughes, who is a member of a prominent rugby league football family. With my encouragement, Chris had spent some time in America studying and researching head-and-neck surgery, particularly cancers in the head and neck. He returned to Australia as a well-trained head-and-neck surgeon but decided that he would like to establish a foundation to raise funds to support young people wishing to do research in cancer either in Australia or abroad. He recognised the difficulty of obtaining financial support from the established cancer authorities. As he and his brothers, Jack and Tim, moved in the circles of Australia's most prominent sportsmen and sportswomen, he gained the support of many sportsmen and sportswomen to establish 'The Sporting Chance Foundation for Cancer Research'. Members included such sportspeople as Raelene Boyle (Olympic medallist and cancer survivor), Reg Gasnier (champion rugby league player), Mark Taylor (Australian cricket captain), Rob Skilton (champion Australian rules player) and Gai Waterhouse (champion racehorse trainer). Other interested parties were Johnny Raper (champion rugby league player), Bart Cummings (champion racehorse trainer), Alan Jones (formerly Australia's most successful Australian rugby coach and now leading broadcaster), the late Peter Brock (champion racing car driver) and Michael Sullivan (leading bookmaker). Chris honoured me by asking me to be the foundation chairman of this group and later to accept a directorship for as long as I felt I was able to help. With the support of many leading business people and companies (especially KPMG), this foundation has raised many thousands of dollars, every dollar of which has been used to support cancer research.

Chapter 11

Kurmond Again

I will always remember our little old house in Kurmond as home. Other houses I have lived in have never been quite the same. Kurmond was the place in the world where I most wanted to be, where I most belonged. Even though the house was very humble nowhere else held such treasured memories and provided such constant unconditional love. It was my sanctuary to which I hoped to return and retire one day. I dreamed of sharing my happy childhood memories with Sheilagh and our children and grandchildren and the families of my brothers and sisters.

Sadly it could never be. The timbers in our house grew old and fragile and our much loved home was eventually replaced by a modern mansion. To this very day my most constant dream involves this home. In the dream I am walking home from the train through the bush only to discover that our house is no longer ours, and my Mum and Dad are no longer there. Then I wake, always with a feeling of sadness and regret.

In many ways I feel sorry for today's children and the over-concern so many parents have with their security and safety: a concern that means children are kept inside in front of televisions and computers for too much of their time. As children we always had something constructive to do. There were cows to be milked, chooks to be fed, wood to be chopped, water to be pumped, a fuel stove to get started, or a primus stove to boil water for tea. And there was always Dad's workshop to make things in and a big enough garden in which to grow things. If there were no chores that needed to be done there was always cricket or tennis on the dirt road nearby, camping in the bush, bikes or horses to be ridden, and dams and creeks to swim or fish in.

Living in a close-knit family taught me nothing about politics or the need to be less than frank and open in making agreements. Nor did I learn how to lobby to promote my own cause in competition with others. But I did learn from my parents the satisfaction gained from being in a position to help others, particularly the sick, and the value of being part of a close-knit family. These are values I would not exchange for wealth or power.

I suppose one good thing that came out of the demise of our house in Kurmond was the impetus it gave me to write this book. I didn't want my home, my mum and dad and my favourite things to be forgotten, and I especially wanted my children and grandchildren to know about them and some of the adventures, challenges and special people in my life.

Finally I am honoured to quote from a letter I found that my mother wrote to her father on my seventh birthday: 'I don't imagine any of my children will be especially clever but I do want them to grow to be good citizens and helpful to all others irrespective of race, creed or social status.'

My response goes something like this: 'We haven't always lived up to all of your hopes, Mum, but all of my brothers and sisters and their families fulfilled most of your dreams, and although we all sometimes fall short of what you would have wished, I think you and Dad would have been pleased with some of the outcomes that flowed from the example you taught us. I am very proud, not only of my children and grandchildren, who are simply gorgeous, but of every one of my siblings and their families.'

When I retired from my university position in 1993, my older brother Stan, helped by my younger brother Bruce, and their families, arranged a wonderful weekend gathering on Stan's farm in Mudgee. They were joined by my sisters Evelyn, Joyce and Elaine who came with members of their families. To add to my delight Stan had also invited a number of my closest friends from school, university and Sydney Hospital. It was a wonderful weekend. It was on that occasion that in a speech Stan reminded us all that the family often referred to me as 'The Professor', even when I was at primary school. What a pity we don't still have that crystal ball!

Sadly they are not all with us now: Joyce, Heather, Stan and Bruce have since died, but I am blessed to have had wonderful brothers and sisters who always encouraged and supported me in my work, all having learnt their values from the example set by our Mum and Dad. They tried to show us what was right, not what might be expedient for wealth, fame, power or glory. They taught us that we should be most concerned to do our best for our family, our friends, our community and our country, as well as communities of every race, colour, creed or social status, wherever they might be.

After all these years of travel, meeting people from other countries, traditions and faiths and a strong Christian upbringing from devoted parents, I have a very strong religious faith. Although not an active member of any one traditional religion, I believe that to see the world and all its beauty, its creatures, its poetry, music, its mysteries, human imagination, love and thought; to see the innocence and beauty in the eyes of children, the incomprehensible minuteness of the atom and the even more incomprehensible vastness of the universe, and not accept that there is a wonderful creative power and wisdom behind it all, is ignoring the obvious. There must be some unimaginably great design and designer behind it all, which most religions refer to as God.

Where I part company with traditional religions is that I can't accept that any one religion has exclusive knowledge of God. There is good in all religions that may be summed up in the simple teachings of Jesus, 'love thy neighbour' and 'do unto others as you would have them do unto you'. The 'ten commandments' set a wonderful standard for human living. The only religions that I am sure are wrong are those that believe they are the only one that is right and are intolerant of anyone who believes anything else.

My old headmaster, Mr Armstrong, might not approve of my grammar but I would definitely say to my parents: 'You done good'.

Acknowledgements

Family and friends

I wish to acknowledge the help of many members of my family and extended family for advice and help in the writing of this book. My son Peter and my niece Dorothy Kallis first suggested that I should write my memoirs. My wife, Sheilagh, my daughter Jenny, my sister-in-law Thelma, and my friends Pauline Doherty, Len Fienberg, Jack and Lynette Skipper, Bruce Herriot, and Sol Posen, Sheilagh's sisters Patricia and Petra, her aunt Jeanne, her nephews Alex Reilly and John Reeve and her brother-in law Doug Howarth, all read the manuscript at various stages and gave helpful advice. I owe a special debt to professional editors Patti Miller and Anthony Reeder who edited the final manuscript. Thanks also to Kathy Sharrad of Wakefield Press for copy editing. I asked my close colleague and good friend, the late Emeritus Professor Gerry Milton, to read the manuscript in case he disagreed with any of the more controversial aspects of the book. Gerry reassured me that, in his opinion, the book was factually honest and correct. Former Chairman of the Australian Medical Association, Sir Keith Jones, also kindly read the manuscript and supported my recollections of events of years past.

I am particularly grateful to Sydney University's Emeritus Professor Ruthven Blackburn, who not only read the manuscript but also helped me to correct and expand some of the detail of events of those somewhat tumultuous years.

I am grateful to the late Mr Reg Money of Sydney Hospital and Mr Ray Barbour, and the late Bob Haynes and colleagues of the Royal Prince Alfred Hospital Audio-visual Departments and Mr Michael Chapman of the Royal Prince Alfred Haematology Department for the clinical photographs. I also thank my school friend, Philip Chapman, for some of the schooldays photographs. Permission to print photographs of 'Pansy' and the flooded bridge at North Richmond taken by I.K. Winney, N.J. Reed and M. Reberger was kindly given by the Tourist Railway Association of Kurrajong. Permission to print the photograph of 'Pansy' crossing the bridge at

North Richmond was kindly granted by Hawkesbury Municipal Library from their collection (number 002199).

I particularly thank my dear wife Sheilagh, who has always understood why I needed to write this book and has supported me at every stage of its production.

Professional gratitude

I especially acknowledge the help and comradeship of colleagues in the medical profession both in Australia and overseas. With very few exceptions colleagues are always willing to lend a hand or give a word of advice, either over a medical or a private matter.

If I had my life to live over I would certainly still have the same ambition I had as a five-year-old. I would still want to be a member of this profession like the doctors in Germany who looked after my dad after he had been given up for dead on that battlefield in France, and like the doctors who continued to care for him so well after his repatriation to Australia and settlement in Kurmond. The profession in which, with very few exceptions the world over, each member is primarily dedicated to doing his or her best for the well-being of the sick, the injured, and those suffering in the community.

APPENDIX

Special Clinical Features of Surgical Oncology

Dedication to cancer patients

We do have very good cancer services in Sydney, and one of the world's best and most comprehensive departments of surgery but Sydney still needs an independent surgical oncology unit. Such a unit, with appropriate staff and facilities, would allow continued research and progress integrating surgery with chemotherapy and radiotherapy and some cancer patients could be given even better and more effective care. Australia should then be able to regain the world leadership we once had in this specialised area of cancer care and research.

A 'kid from Kurmond' can do so much, but I have not had the lobbying skills, the time, the smooth talking skills nor the patience, to match the 'castle-building' of others in medicine who have spent time writing programs, developing political contacts, seeing and supporting important power-broking people in their ambitions, but it is clear that to establish a balanced first rate comprehensive cancer centre a widely experienced and dedicated university department of surgical oncology is mandatory. Without it any centre will not be balanced, as all the skills of modern complex integrated cancer management will not be represented. This is still lacking in Sydney and if Sydney University authorities agree I plan to dedicate royalties from the sale of this book and all my other books to the establishment of such a chair to be known as the Dorys and Hedley Stephens Chair of Surgical Oncology in honour of my parents without whose unfailing love and encouragement this work would not have been established in our medical school.

WARNING

Not every reader will want to see photographs illustrating the sort of work my unit was undertaking that proved to be of worldwide interest. However I will add this appendix to show just a few photographic examples of what, with the help and co-operation of Dr Hambly, Professor Gunz, Dr Stan McCarthy and Dr Bill Marsden and a number of specialist nurses (mentioned previously), my unit was able to achieve under the conditions of our work together in Sydney Hospital and later in the Royal Prince Alfred Hospital.

Clinical lessons to be learnt

Very close and diligent supervision is needed otherwise mistakes will be made.

Some people have used intra-arterial chemotherapy without first learning the importance of keeping a close vigil to be sure that the cannula is still in the right position and has not slipped into an artery supplying blood to another tissue instead of the cancer. Figure 15 in the Appendix (page 177) shows damage in tissues in a patient's thigh was because nobody had noticed that the chemotherapy had been flowing into the wrong branch of the artery into which it had originally been placed.

Without the services of well trained, dedicated, experienced nurses to constantly watch for such errors intra-arterial infusions of chemotherapy can cause such problems. This patient had been treated in another hospital by a medical team not experienced in administering chemotherapy by intra-arterial infusion. If an experienced oncologist or a good nurse oncologist had closely watched this patient it would have been obvious that in this area, that was not near the cancer, the skin was becoming red and inflamed. The position of the cannula in the artery should then have been changed before this serious damage had occurred. The damage done to the tissues in this patient's thigh is an indication of the damage that should have been done to the cancer had the cannula been in the right place, that is in the artery directly supplying blood to the cancer.

Clinical summary

When properly and safely applied the surgical oncology techniques illustrated in the Appendix pages 165–177 can be invaluable for treating appropriate patients but the work does require a particularly experienced and dedicated team of doctors and nurses, otherwise mistakes will be made. The clinical illustrations represent advances made in my unit at Sydney Hospital between 1969 and 1984 when we were world leaders in this field. Further developments, especially in orthopaedic oncology, were made in the Royal Prince Alfred hospital with Professor Bill Marsden, Professor Richard Fox, Dr (now Professor) Stan McCarthy and vascular radiologist Dr Richard Waugh. Progress continues in orthopaedic oncology and gynaecologic oncology under the direction of Dr Paul Stalley and Professor Jonathan Carter. However without the support of a well funded university department of surgical oncology the general world leadership in more areas cannot be regained. Our city, our state and our country deserve such a team particularly because much of this work was developed in Sydney.

Footnote

I should make it clear that the great majority of patients under my care for cancers were treated by traditional means just as they would have been treated by other surgeons. Thus most were treated by surgical excision with or without follow-up radiotherapy and/or chemotherapy. Most patients did not need prolonged and complicated integrated treatment schedules to achieve best results.

However about 20% of all my patients were referred by other surgeons and specialists who considered cure of their cancers would be unlikely by any standard treatment or at least without mutilation such as radical head and neck surgery requiring major reconstruction (and still with a low incidence of cure), or limb amputation.

The overall numbers of such patients in any one medical practice are very small; and still small in number in any one surgical practice. However, especially in Sydney Hospital, my practice had an unusually high number of such patients, simply because it was the only unit that specialised in such integrated treatment, and our results impressed our colleagues who were able to see our work first hand and took a close interest in it. There was no rival unit, neither medical nor surgical.

In developing Surgical Oncology in Sydney Hospital not only did I have encouraging support of colleagues, but excellent nurses who were truly dedicated to the special nature of their work. Also in Sydney Hospital there was no restriction of use of hospital beds for these, relatively small, numbers of patients. Clinical colleagues and supporting staff, as well as the medical superintendent and administrative staff, were able to see that for those who did need integrated treatment our results were very rewarding.

The situation was not same in the larger Royal Prince Alfred Hospital with territorial rivalries where people with cancer had usually been treated by a surgeon or a radiotherapist and because of development of increasing numbers of effective and complex anti-cancer drugs a medical oncology unit had become established.

Over the years people with potentially curable cancers have customarily been referred to a surgeon and people with non-operable cancers had usually been referred to a radiotherapist. Radiotherapists also treated people who had had a cancer removed surgically but some doubt existed as to whether the cancer had been totally removed.

In the early days of chemotherapy only people with widespread or non-resectable cancers were referred to medical oncologists but as more effective and more complex anti-cancer drugs became available medical oncologists became interested in treating increasing numbers of cancer patients.

Thus three virtually competing cancer treatment specialty units evolved, between which, at least in the early days, there was little co-operation or integration.

Things have now changed; there is now much more of a cooperative team approach in managing difficult cancer problems but the value, the techniques and skills of integrating regional chemotherapy to reduce locally advanced cancers to curable proportions before radiotherapy and/or surgery, is now largely a lost art. It seems that in Australia these techniques requiring technical skills of surgeons or vascular radiologists to correctly place intra-arterial cannulas, constant vigil of dedicated nurses to observe reactions of the tumours and ensure correct flow of drugs to where they are needed, and patience and expense of hospital inpatient care for some weeks, have been largely lost in present-day hospital economic conditions. For these relatively small numbers of patients, quantity and cost of care has taken precedence over quality of care.

An update on simultaneous chemo/radiotherapy

In treating locally advanced cancers with intra-arterial induction chemotherapy, the intra-arterial infusion has been given over a slow infusion period of up to five or six weeks and then a break of three weeks before commencing radiotherapy. Provided this is closely monitored it has been very effective treatment for a broad range of locally advanced cancers, such as those illustrated in this book. However it is prolonged and expensive in length of hospital bed stay.

More recently simultaneous combined chemotherapy and radiotherapy has been used with the hope of achieving similar results in controlling locally advanced cancers. These treatment programs are simpler to deliver as the chemotherapy is usually given systemically. The chemotherapy sensitises the cancer cells, as well as other cells, to radiotherapy, making the local radiotherapy more effective. However all cells in the radiation fields are made more sensitive to the radiotherapy so that not only is the cancer damaged so too are normal cells in the irradiated region. The doses of chemotherapy and radiotherapy are therefore more critical between not being sufficient to achieve the desired effect on the cancer on the one hand or, on the other hand, causing potentially dangerous damage to surrounding tissues such as nearby arteries and underlying bone (particularly the mandible or maxilla in the case of head-and-neck cancers). Most safe and effective combinations are still being studied in many situations.

If we had a department of surgical oncology it would now be leading in this field of integrated treatment for locally advanced cancers, rather than waiting for information to come from overseas institutions.

Clinical acknowledgements

I wish to acknowledge people who assisted in achieving the results of treatment at Sydney Hospital here demonstrated.

Radiotherapist – the late Colin Hambly.
Haematologist and Oncologist – the late Fred Gunz.
Pathologist – Stan McCarthy.
Medical Superintendents: the late Norman Rose, Bruce Herriott, Ron Beasley, the late John Watson and the late Vicky Pearson. Each of these superintendents always made a bed or beds available for as long as needed for the best care of my patients. They were aware of my original study of 'Outpatient Surgery' and knew full well that I preferred to get my patients up and about and home as soon as possible. They knew that I would not keep patients in hospital for prolonged treatment unless this was necessary to achieve best results.
Radiologists – James Wright, John Cashman, Bruce Roberts and Michael Wong.
Surgical Assistant – Ian Kalnins.
Research Fellow – Gary Harker.
Registrars – Alf Lewis, Bala Duraiappah, the late Ian Isaacs, Kevin Hellestrand, Ian Wechsler, John Milverton, Peter Endrey-Walder, Andrew Gatenby, Hari Kapila, Paul Crea, Brett Adam.
Resident Medical Officers – Max Williams, Bill Buddee, Peter Hunter, Elenor Sebel, Alex Vrjosseck, Kevin Lawrenson, Fred Wechsler, Warwick Gordon-Smith, Michael Moont, Robert Dickinson, the late Michael Bender, David Pennington, Robin Fitsimons, Greg Stewart, Georgina Kourt, Michael Morris, Alice Killen.

I am also much indebted to a number of very dedicated nurse oncologists – Sue Cruikshank, Jenny Dempsy, Amy Teoh and Rosemary Farrell at Sydney Hospital and later at the Royal Prince Alfred Hospital Gabrielle Prest, Leanne Watson, Jenene Bell the late Cheryl Daley. My Sydney Hospital secretary, Maggie Glasgow, was most loyal and helpful in her assistance.

Later in the Royal Prince Alfred Hospital, the assistance was appreciated of Richard Waugh (Senior Radiologist) and Surgical Registrars Philip Walker, James Gallagher, Chris Hughes, Michael Solomon, Kirwin Shannon and the late Greg Monaghan.

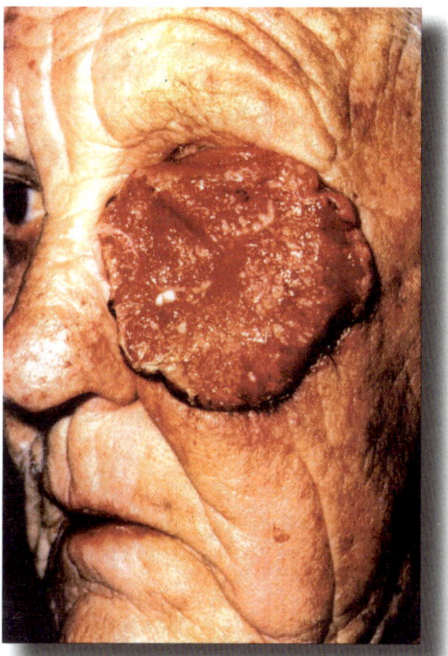

1 (a) Photograph of a cancer growing over the left eye of a ninety year-old woman. This cancer had never been treated before she was first referred to our Sydney Hospital unit.

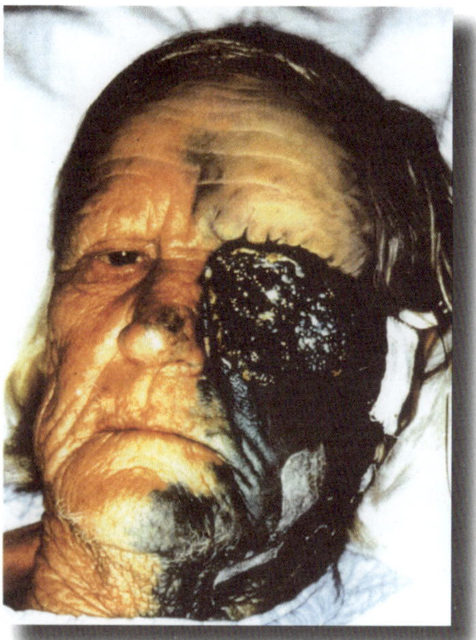

1 (b) A blue dye injected into the artery suppling blood to the left side of her face confirmed that the cancer would get a greater concentration of chemotherapy when chemotherapy was infused into this artery.

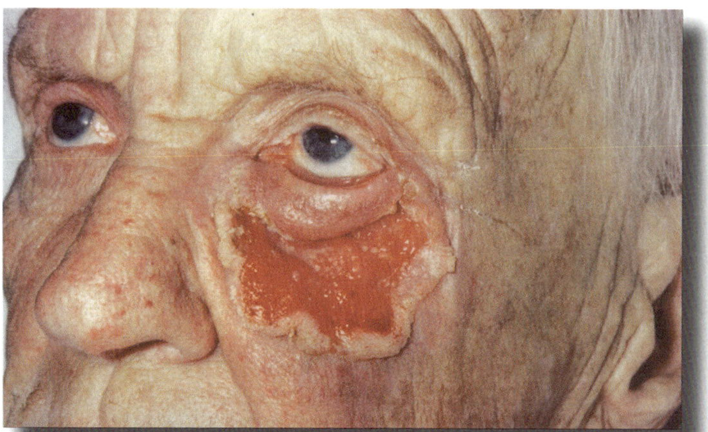

1 (c) After four weeks of continuous chemotherapy infused into this artery, the cancer was much smaller and the lady could see again. She was satisfied with this result as she could see again, but at the age of ninety she declined any further treatment.

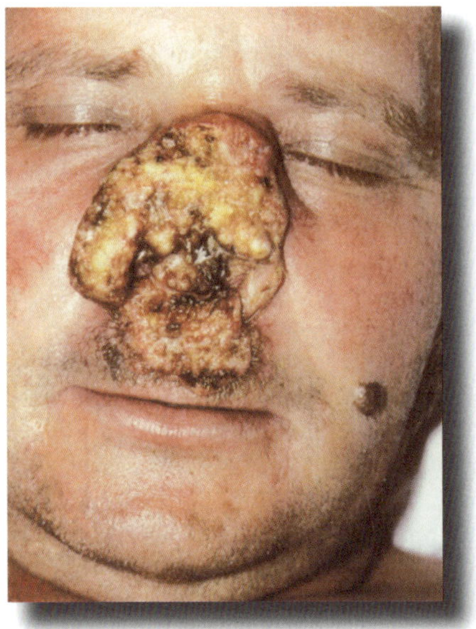

2 (a) This man had neglected this cancer that was destroying his nose.

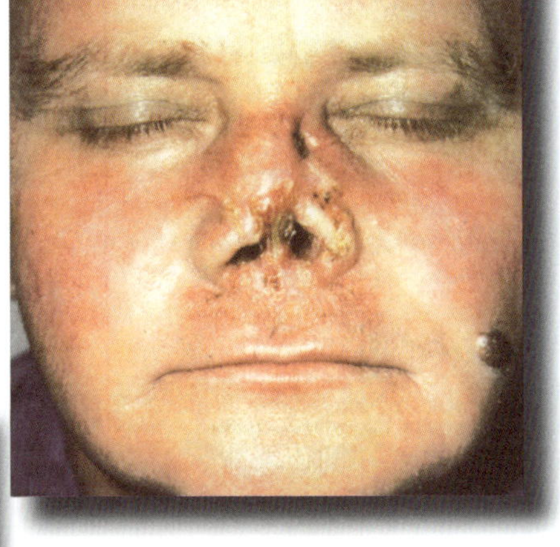

2 (b) After five weeks chemotherapy infused into the arteries supplying blood to his face (one on each side) the cancer had regressed considerably to allow following radiotherapy to be very effective.

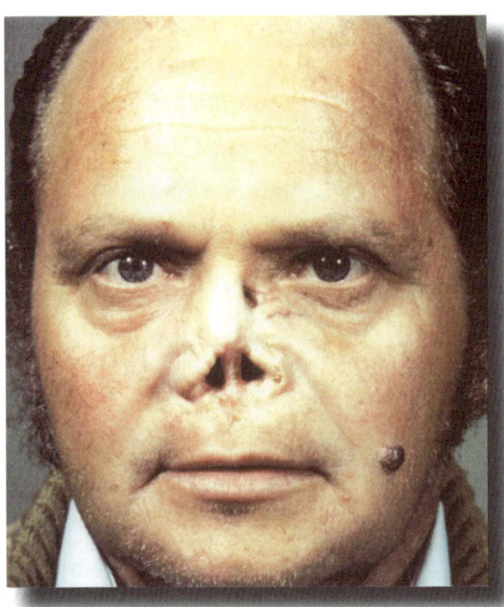

2 (c) After completion of radiotherapy there was no longer any cancer, but quite a deformity of his nose. After a further two years when there was no recurrence of his cancer his nose was reconstructed by plastic surgery. When last seen 5 years later he was well and had not had any evidence of cancer.

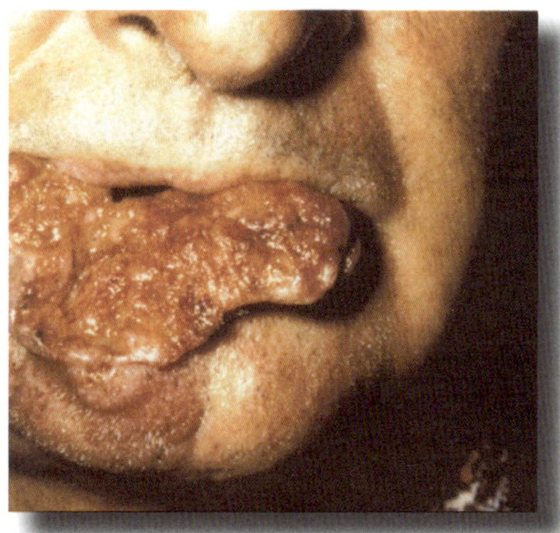

3 (a) This man presented with this large cancer of his lower lip. It had not had any previous treatment.

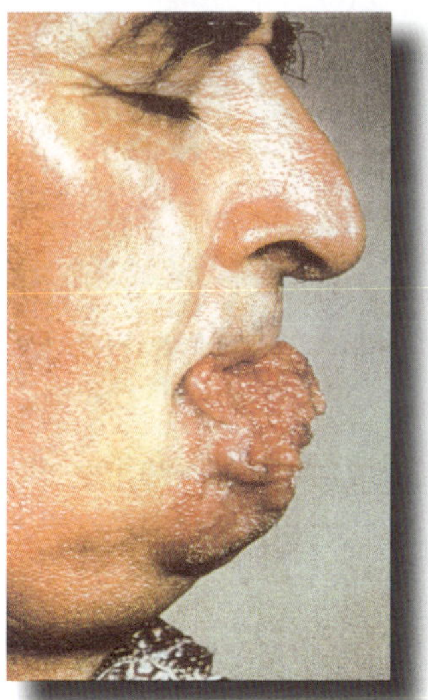

3 (b) The cancer not only involved the whole of his lower lip it had also spread into enlarged lymph nodes in the right side of his neck.

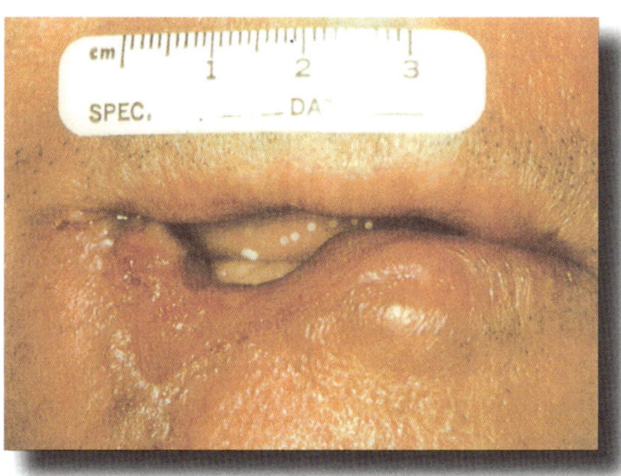

3 (c) After five weeks of continuous infusion into the arteries on both sides of his neck, the cancer of his lip was much smaller, as were the enlarged lymph nodes in his neck.

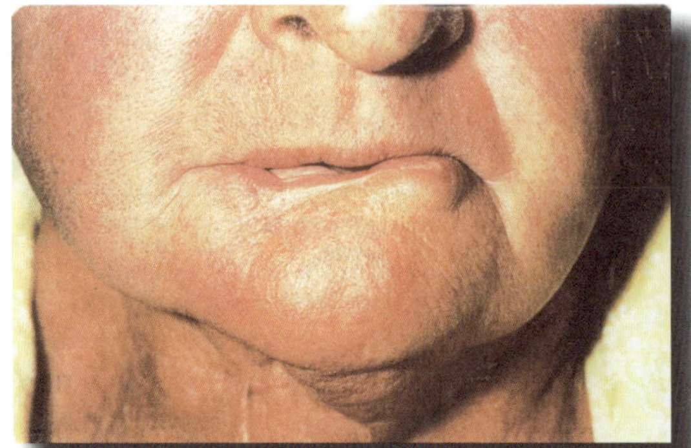

3 (d) Three weeks later radiotherapy was commenced. The final result showed no evidence of cancer in his lip.

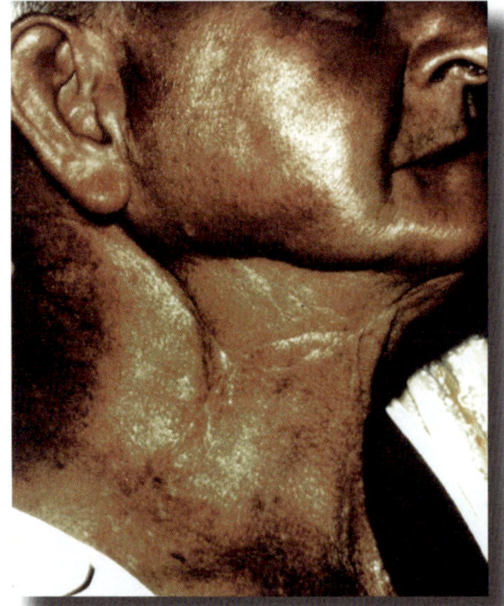

3 (e) The lymph nodes in the right side of his neck were smaller but they were still enlarged. I therefore resected all the lymph nodes from the right side of his neck (an operation called a block dissection of lymph nodes). This photograph shows the scars on his neck six months later. There was no evidence of any further cancer.

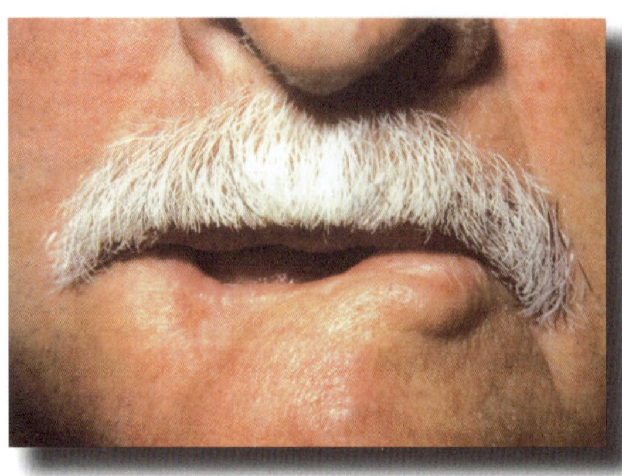

3 (f) Like so many patients who wait for so long to first seek treatment, he did not keep his 'follow-up' appointments, but I happened to bump into him at a horse race meeting twelve years later. He remained well and I arranged to have this photograph taken.

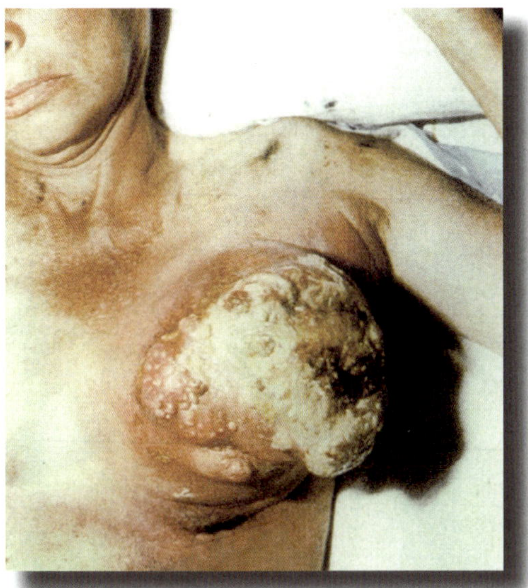

4 (a) The woman with this huge bleeding, smelling breast cancer was an alcoholic and had never before consulted a doctor when she was brought to Sydney Hospital by ambulance. We inserted a cannula into the artery in the lower neck (the subclavian artery) that supplied the breast with blood and treated her with intra-arterial chemotherapy.

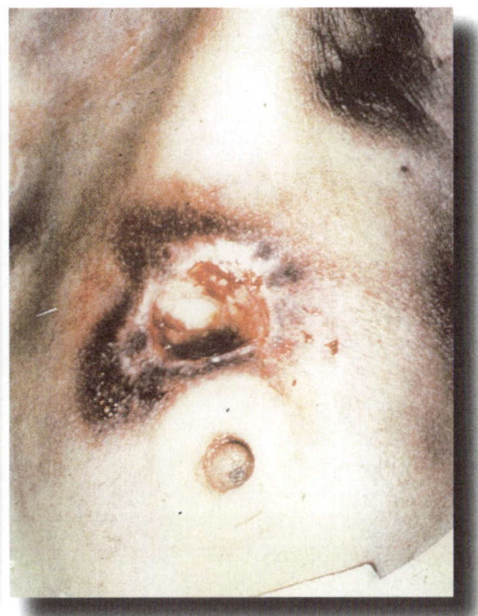

4 (b) After a month of treatment the cancer had regressed.

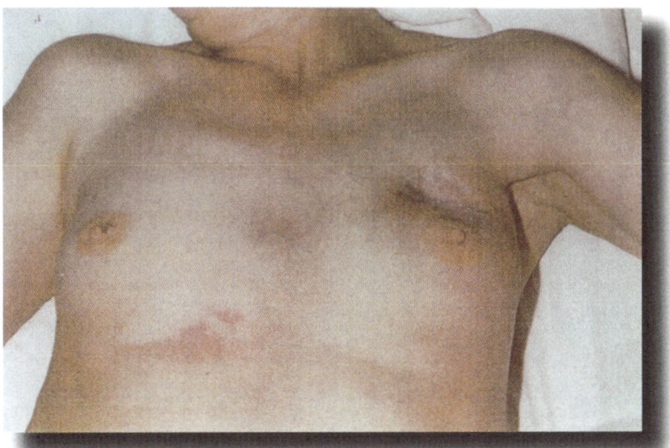

4 (c): After a break of three weeks Dr Colin Hambly treated her with radiotherapy and the cancer completely disappeared from her breast. We knew that she had some liver metastases, but they were not causing her pain, bleeding and discomfort as the breast had been. She died two years later with liver metastases but there was no further recurrence in her breast.

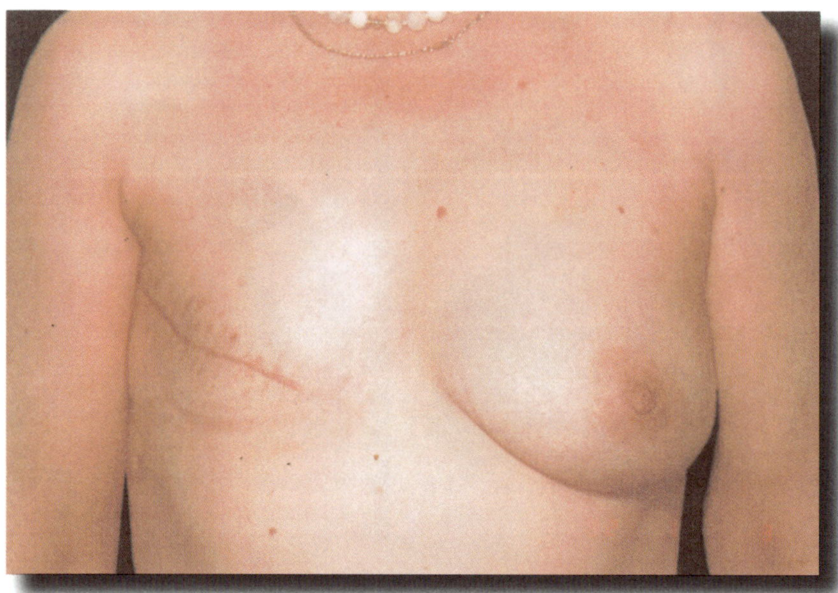

5 (a) and 5(b): Photographs illustrating a brilliant breast reconstruction performed by Dr David Pennington, head of the plastic and reconstruction unit at the Royal Prince Alfred Hospital. I am proud to say that David Pennington was once the surgical registrar in training in my unit in Sydney Hospital.

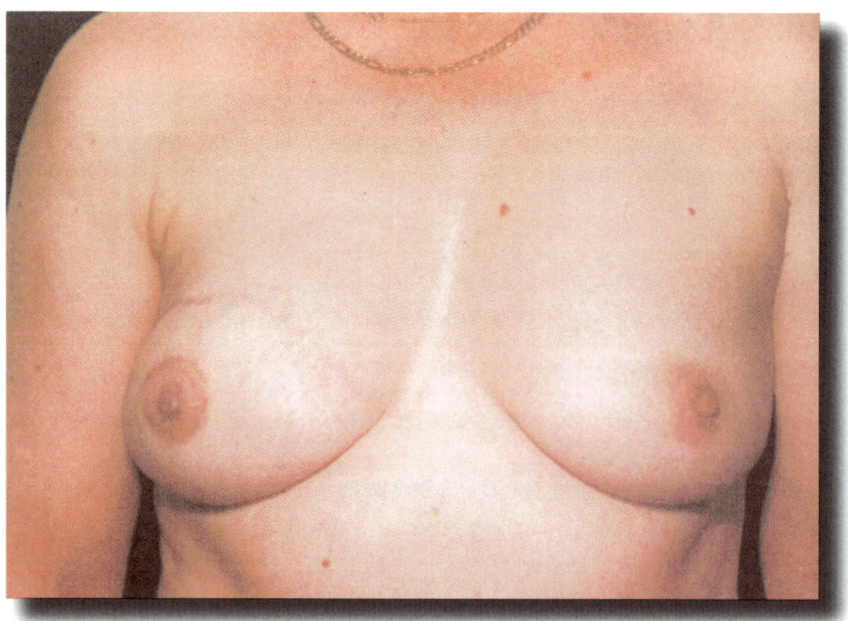

5 (b)

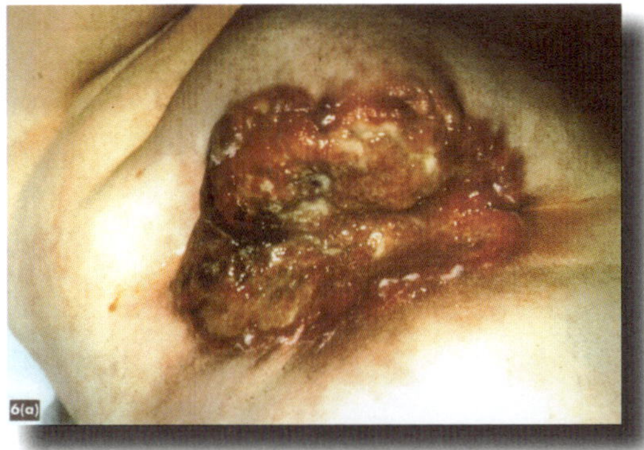

6 (a) Photograph of an advanced cancer in right breast of a fifty-six year-old woman. It had not been treated previously but a cancer of this size would be most unlikely to be cured by surgery or by radiotherapy.

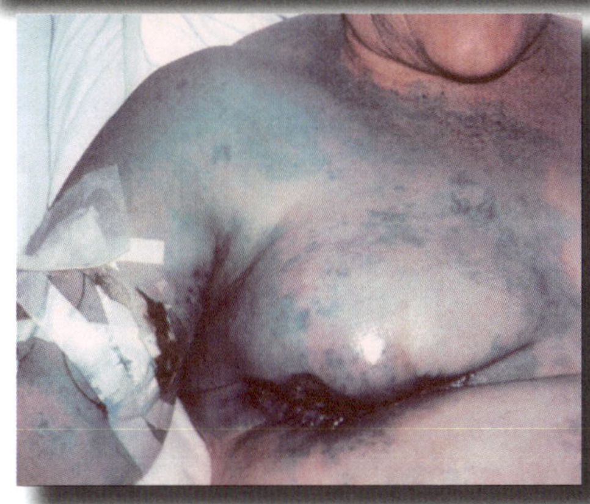

6 (b) This photograph, taken after blue dye was injected into a small cannula that had been inserted into the artery supplying blood to the cancer, confirmed that anti-cancer drugs infused into this cannula would be most concentrated in the cancer and surrounding tissues.

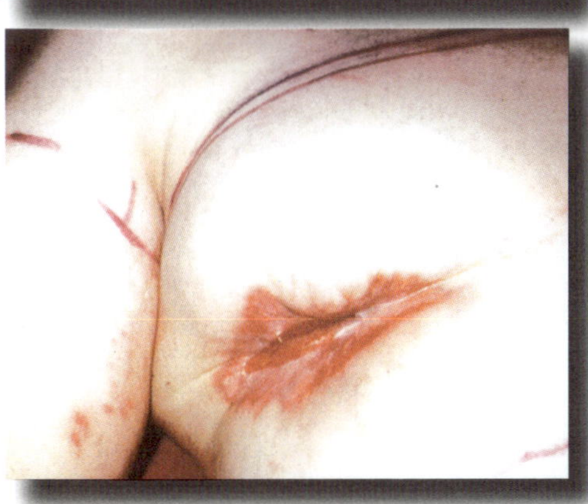

6 (c) After five weeks of continuous intra-arterial chemotherapy the cancer had regressed considerably.

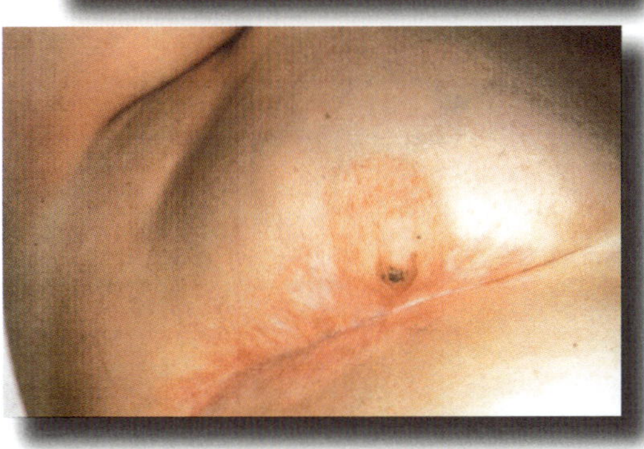

6 (d) After radiotherapy administered by Dr Hambly (commencing three weeks after completion of chemotherapy) the cancer had completely responded. Three months later this scar remained but there was no evidence of residual cancer. First treated in 1980 this lady continued to be well for five years before cancer secondaries in her liver became evident. To reduce the risk of later recurrence of cancer in the breast or development of metastases we now always recommend removal of the breast and post-operative 'adjuvant chemotherapy' as a routine in such advanced cases.

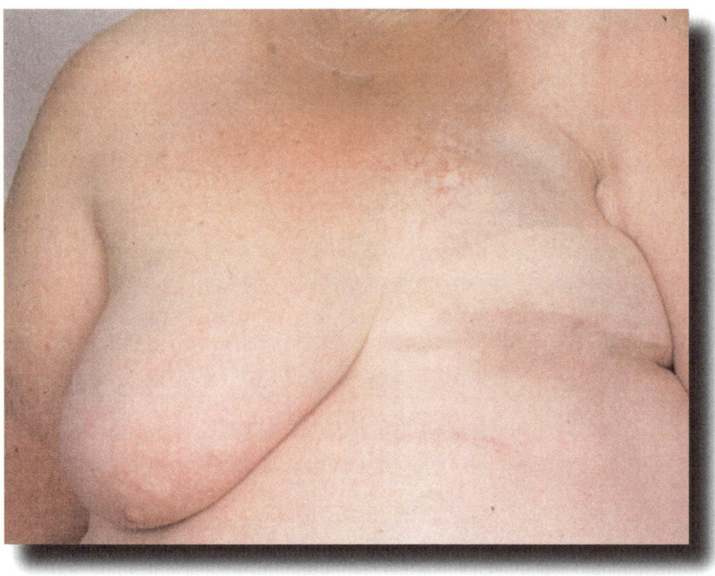

7 In 1982 a forty eight year old lady presented with a seven cm inflammatory type medullary carcinoma in her left breast. It was similar to the cancer seen in Figure 6(a). The cancer was fixed to overlying red skin and deep tissues. It was treated with a similar regimen as was used in the patient seen in Figure 6(a).

The mass much reduced after intra-arterial chemotherapy and further resolved after radiotherapy but there remained thickened tissue attached to skin in the region of the original cancer. This tissue was widely resected and the resulting defect was repaired by a full thickness rotation flap taken from over her back of shoulder muscle (latissimus dorsi muscle). No viable cancer cells were found in the resected fibrous tissue. She was then treated with systemic chemotherapy for four months. The photograph (Figure 7) shows the end result. The patient remains well and free from cancer at the time of writing, which is twenty-seven years after her treatment.

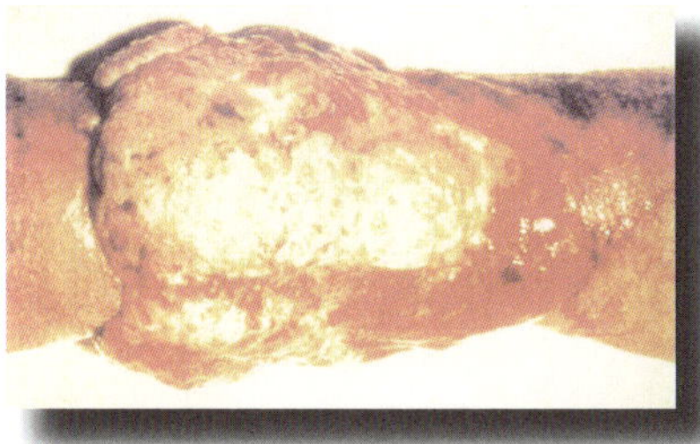

8 (a) This untreated cancer completely surrounded the lower right forearm of this 60 year-old oyster farmer. There were also enlarged lymph nodes with cancer spread in his armpit. A surgeon had advised him to have his arm and shoulder amputated but the patient refused. This was in 1973. The surgeon then referred him to our clinic at Sydney Hospital to see what we could do.

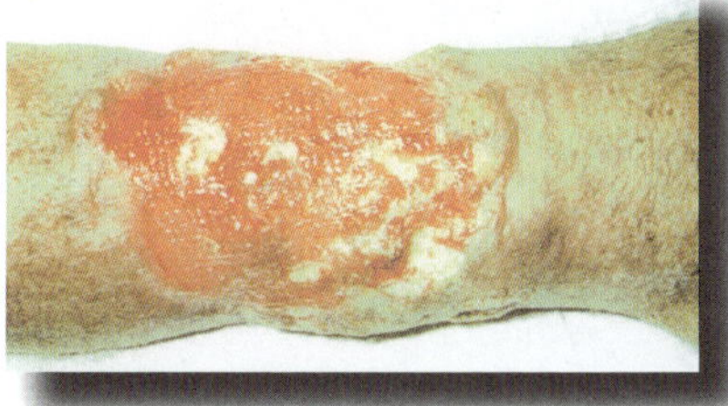

8 (b) With a small operation I inserted a cannula into the main artery that supplied blood to the whole upper limb including the armpit nodes. After five weeks of continuous slow chemotherapy infusion the cancer had regressed leaving a shallow ulcer still containing some cancer cells.

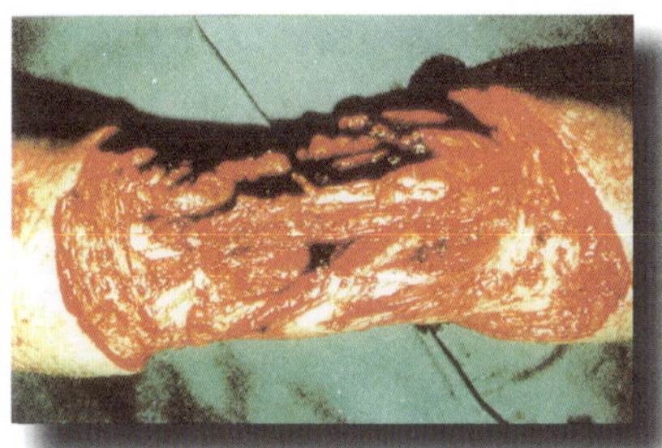

8 (c) After I had resected the residual ulcer containing cancer cells some tendons and bone were exposed in the open wound. This needed more than an ordinary split skin graft to allow good healing and a useful functioning arm.

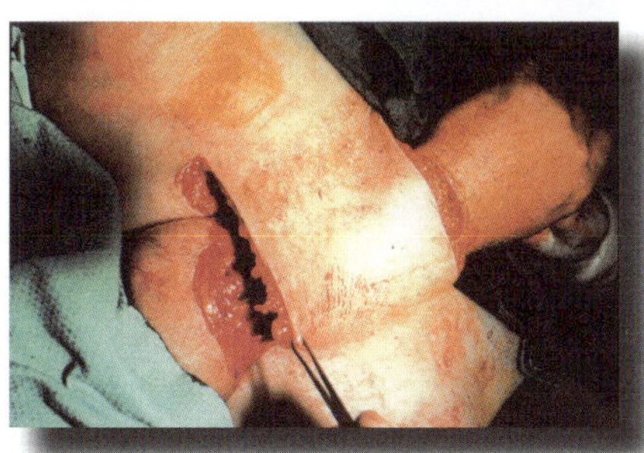

8 (d) & 8 (e) To get full thickness skin cover with some protective fat I made a bridge of skin in his lower abdomen and buried the arm in it so covering the wound, tendons and bone. After four weeks the full thickness abdominal wall skin was growing over the wound so it was detached from his abdomen and a split skin graft was applied to the open abdominal wound from which the abdominal skin had been taken. I then resected the lymph nodes in the armpit. These were much smaller but still contained some cancer cells.

The second photo shows the final result one year later. For twelve years this man always brought me a bucket of oysters when he came to see me on follow-up visits. He claimed that I deserved it not only for saving his arm but also whenever he went to his local village pub someone would always want to see his arm covered by abdominal skin and his abdomen with a split skin graft. He was always supplied with free beers to demonstrate this.

I was sorry to learn that this delightful man died after a heart attack 15 years after his operation but was pleased to learn from his doctor that he had no evidence of residual cancer.

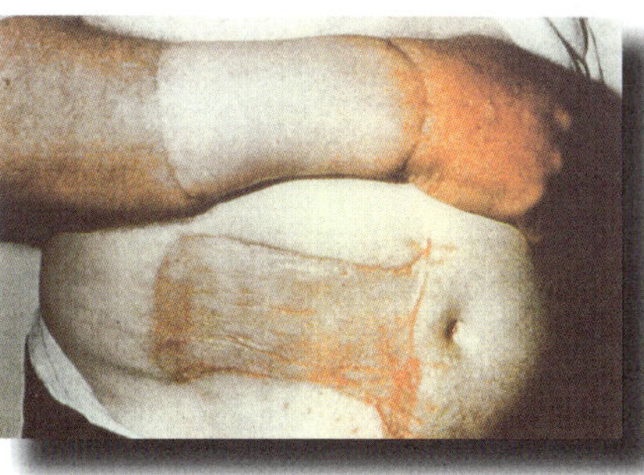

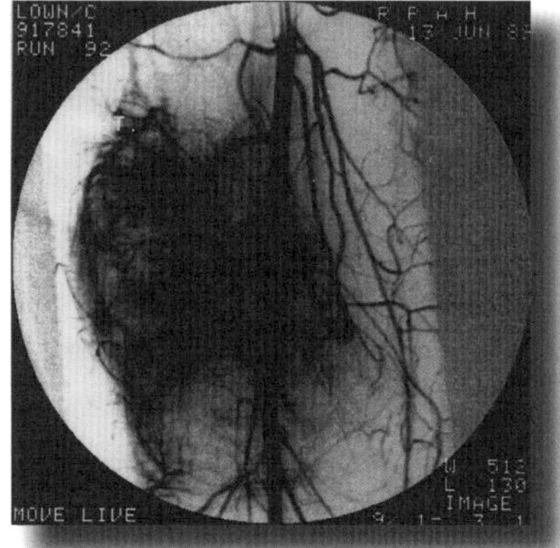

9 (a) before treatment

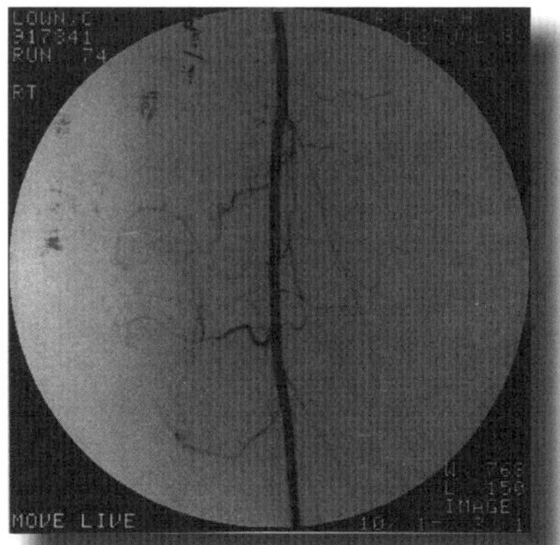

9 (b) after treatment

The series of pictures above and below are before and after angiograms of limb cancers (sarcomas) that I treated at Sydney and The Royal Prince Alfred Hospitals, some with Orthopaedic surgeon the late Professor Bill Marsden. Whenever bone had to be resected and a bone or joint replaced this was done by Professor Marsden. In the Royal Prince Alfred Hospital Dr Richard Waugh in the Radiology Department inserted the intra-arterial cannulas into the supplying arteries without need for an operation.

Pathologist, Dr Stan McCarthy, was another important member of our team as he not only advised us as to exactly what sort of cancer we were dealing with but what response there had been to the chemotherapy.

The illustrations on the left show the vascularity of the cancer lumps served by the major artery in the lower limb. The illustrations on the right show that after intra-arterial chemotherapy for three weeks not only had the cancer lumps regressed but the small blood vessels supplying the cancer had disappeared. These reduced cancers were now easily resected without the limb amputations that had originally been recommended.

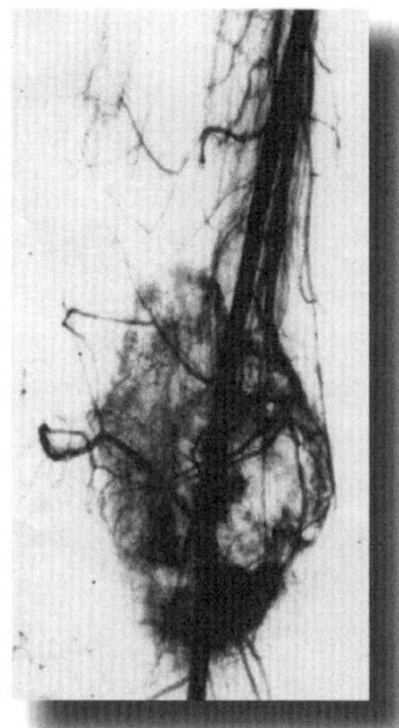

9 (c) Before treatment

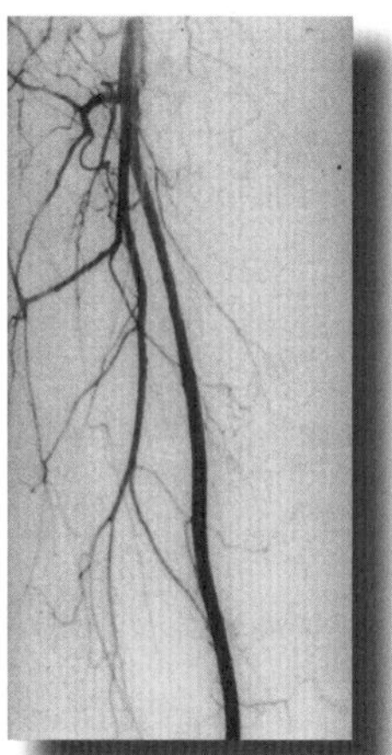

9 (d) After treatment

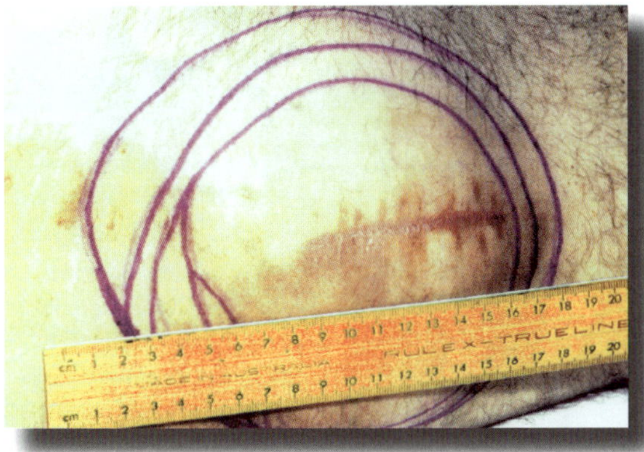

10 (a) The circles around this cancer in a limb (a sarcoma) were drawn at weekly intervals after commencing intra-arterial chemotherapy. The tumour gets smaller as more and more cancer cells in it are destroyed by chemotherapy so that eventually the lump can be excised without need for amputation of the limb.

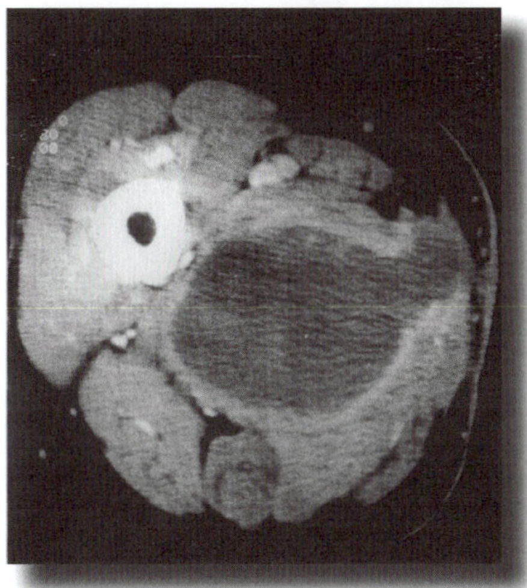

10 (b) Similarly this CT (CAT scan) shows a cancer in a thigh before chemotherapy

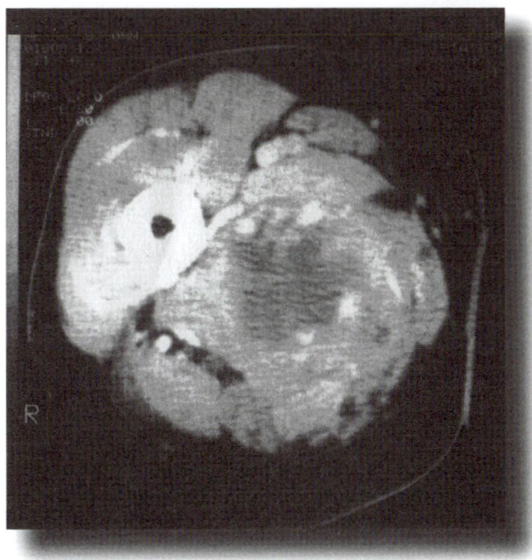

10 (c) Just three weeks after starting intra-arterial chemotherapy the lump is distinctly smaller.

Illustrations showing that most chemotherapy given by intra-arterial infusion should have a greater local impact on a cancer than it does on other tissues

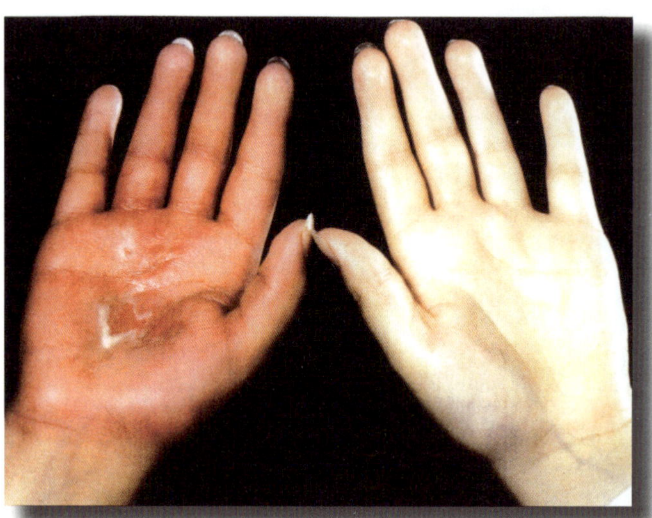

11 As was first noticed many years ago, there is a greater reaction in the tissues supplied with blood by an artery accidentally injected with chemotherapy than if the same dose of the drug had been given into a vein as had been intended. The redness and reaction in this patient's right hand after accidental injection into the artery at the elbow is greater than in her left hand.

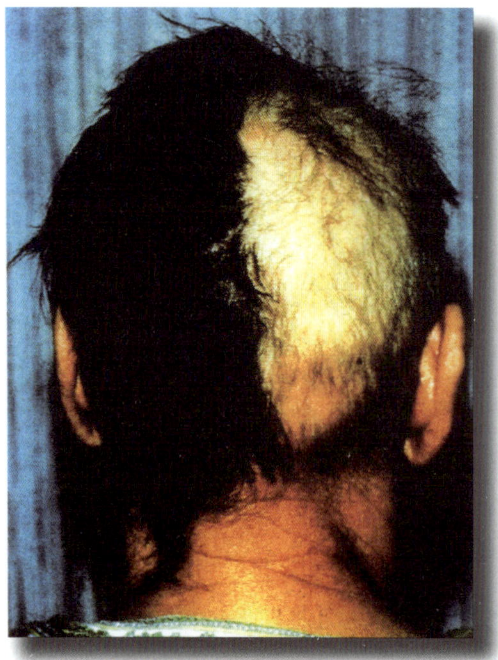

12 In this man, in treating a cancer on the right side of his face by intra-arterial chemotherapy the chemotherapy also infused into the artery supplying blood to the right side of his scalp causing much more hair loss on the right side of his head. This confirms that the chemotherapy was more effective in the tissues supplied by the artery infused. (Hair lost in this way always re-grows some weeks later unless follow-up radiotherapy was given to the scalp region.)

Illustrations showing reasons why intra-arterial chemotherapy is not practised in some cancer clinics – its appropriate use is often poorly understood

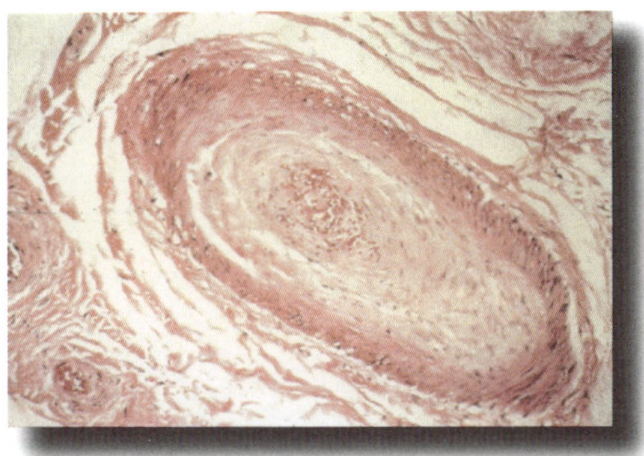

13 During surgery blood vessels are ligated thus reducing the blood supply to cancers that recur in or near the surgical wound. After radiotherapy there is also damage to blood vessels. As this photomicrograph shows most of this small previously irradiated artery is blocked leaving only a small central opening for a small amount of blood containing only a small amount of chemotherapy to flow through to the cancer.

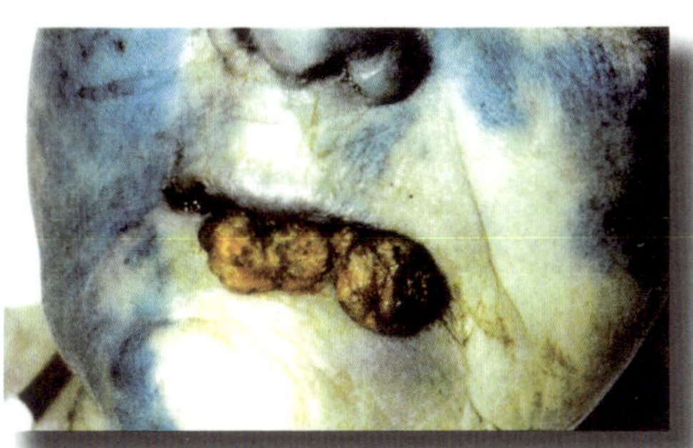

14 This woman had had radiotherapy treatment for a cancer on her lower lip several years previously. Blue dye injected into the arteries on both sides of her head show that the blue flows into the skin of her face except in that part of her face that had previously been irradiated for cancer.

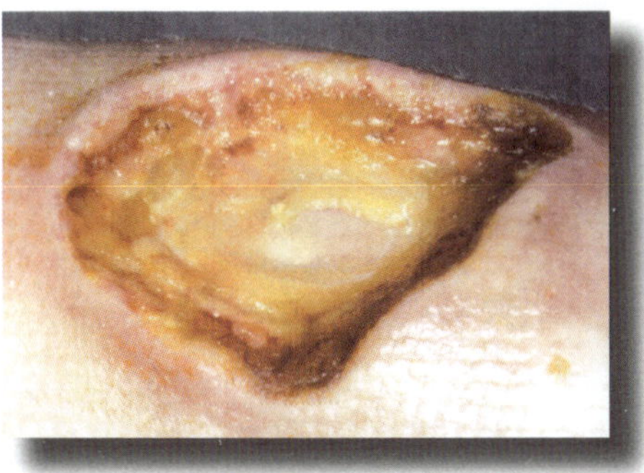

15 Some people have used intra-arterial chemotherapy without first learning the importance of keeping a close vigil to be sure that the cannula is still in the right position and has not slipped into an artery supplying blood to another tissue instead of the cancer. The damage done to normal tissues in this patient's thigh was because nobody had noticed that the chemotherapy had been flowing into the wrong branch of the artery into which it had originally been placed. Without the services of well trained, dedicated, experienced nurses to constantly watch for such errors intra-arterial infusions of chemotherapy can cause such problems.

This patient had been treated in another hospital by a medical team not experienced in administering chemotherapy by intra-arterial infusion. If an oncologist or a good nurse oncologist had closely watched this patient it would have been obvious that in this area, which was not near the cancer, the skin was becoming red and inflamed. The position of the cannula in the artery should then have been changed before this serious damage had been done. The damage done to the tissues in this patient's thigh is an indication of the damage that should have been done to the cancer had the cannula been in the right place, that is in the artery directly supplying blood to the cancer.

Wakefield Press is an independent publishing and
distribution company based in Adelaide, South Australia.
We love good stories and publish beautiful books.
To see our full range of titles, please visit our website at
www.wakefieldpress.com.au.